COLLEGE CRIME PREVENTION AND PERSONAL SAFETY AWARENESS

COLLEGE CRIME PREVENTION
AND
PERSONAL SAFETY AWARENESS

By

MAX L. BROMLEY

Associate Director
Division of Public Safety
University of South Florida
Tampa, Florida

and

LEONARD TERRITO

Professor
Department of Criminology
University of South Florida
Tampa, Florida

CHARLES C THOMAS • PUBLISHER
Springfield • Illinois • U.S.A.

Published and Distributed Throughout the World by

CHARLES C THOMAS • PUBLISHER
2600 South First Street
Springfield, Illinois 62794-9265

© *1990 by* CHARLES C THOMAS • PUBLISHER

ISBN 0-398-05634-X

Library of Congress Catalog Card Number: 89-20239

With THOMAS BOOKS *careful attention is given to all details of manufacturing
and design. It is the Publisher's desire to present books that are satisfactory as to their
physical qualities and artistic possibilities and appropriate for their particular use.*
THOMAS BOOKS *will be true to those laws of quality that assure a good name
and good will.*

Printed in the United States of America
SC-R-3

Library of Congress Cataloging-in-Publication Data

Bromley, Max.
    College crime prevention and personal safety awareness / by Max L.
Bromley and Leonard Territo.
        p. cm.
    Includes bibliographical references.
    ISBN 0-398-05634-X
    1. College students—United States—Crimes against—Prevention.
2. Colleges and universities—United States—Security measures.
3. Campus police—United States. I. Territo, Leonard. II. Title.
HV6250.4.S78B76 1989
362.88′837—dc20   89-20239
                                                          CIP

To our wives, Debbie and Chris

PREFACE

College campuses were once thought to be safe havens where people could send their sons and daughters without having to fear that they might become victims of violent crimes. Unfortunately, on too many college campuses in America today this is simply not true. We now find the types of violent crimes occurring on college campuses that once were confined to the high-crime inner cities. Rape, murder, and robbery have, unfortunately, become commonplace at some American colleges. However, there is much that can be done by college administrators, college law enforcement personnel, and students themselves to reduce the potential for victimization.

The contents of this book will be of specific interest to college administrators and college law enforcement personnel, but, in addition, a number of our chapters will be of interest to students who wish to take steps to provide for their own protection. We have divided the book into six chapters.

In Chapter 1, "Crime on College Campuses," we provide the reader with information regarding issues relative to crimes being committed on college campuses throughout the United States. Specifically, we examine the need to study crimes on campus, review the extent to which crimes are being committed on campuses, perceptions of safety on colleges and universities, and further examine who it is committing the crimes on campuses as well as who is typically victimized. In this chapter we also examine some of the problems involved in attempting to make comparisons between campuses regarding their crime rates as well as the difficulties encountered in making comparisons between campus law enforcement agencies.

While it is often thought that campus law enforcement has exclusive responsibility for crime prevention, such a shortsighted view will not result in the most effective use of other important personnel. For example, in Chapter 2, "Developing A Campus-Wide Approach to Crime Prevention," we discuss the importance of scheduling academic classes and employee work hours in relation to a total crime prevention program. Also, it does no good to have the finest crime prevention program in the world if there is relatively little done to control the distribution of keys to offices and dormitories. Thus, in this chapter, we attempt to outline how university administrators may involve other key departments in the total crime prevention effort.

In Chapter 3, "Critical Issues in Campus Security and Safety," we discuss a series of important issues related to the safety and security on college campuses and discuss how to involve students and campus staff in crime prevention programs such as the use of security teams, security and safety issues in campus residence halls dormitories, residence hall fire safety, alcohol/drug abuse, and the steps campus administrators can take to ensure a proactive approach to campus security and crime prevention.

In Chapter 4, "Off-Campus Apartment Security," we discuss crime prevention issues as they relate to off-campus apartment security. For a variety of reasons, many college students choose to live in apartments off the main college campus. In such areas, one can too often find a number of rapes as well as thefts. In this chapter, we suggest a number of practical ways in which apartments can be made more secure and suggest behaviors that reduce the possibility of students becoming the victims of either personal or property crimes while in or about their apartments.

In Chapter 5, "Preventing Rapes," we discuss what is quite likely the most troublesome issue occurring on American campuses today and that is the issue of rape. This chapter provides very specific crime prevention information about this offense, including an examination of who the typical rapist is, why the crime occurs, what the victim can do to protect herself against assaults, acquaintance rape, and gang rape.

In Chapter 6, "Protecting Student Property and Vehicles on Campus," we discuss the ways in which students may protect both their property and vehicles on campus. We discuss the issue of burglaries on campus as well as the ways in which students can mark their property to make them less attractive to potential thieves. We discuss not only how one can protect the property that typically is stored in their rooms but also how to protect their bicycles and cars from theft.

At the conclusion of all of these chapters, we have provided the reader with a series of suggested security questions to assist in a self-evaluation.

It is our belief that if college administrators, college law enforcement personnel and college students follow most of the very inexpensive, easily implemented, and commonsense suggestions outlined in this book, we will witness a significant decrease in the opportunities for crimes to be committed on college campuses.

M.L.B.
L.T.

ACKNOWLEDGMENTS

In the very early stages of our research efforts for this book, we had some general ideas about the kinds of crime prevention and safety awareness work that was being done by our colleagues on other college and university campuses. However, we knew that in order for this book to be most useful, we needed to obtain very specific information so we could address such serious problems as campus rape, drug abuse, and thefts that were occurring at alarming rates on so many colleges throughout this country. Thus, in our effort to gather as much information as possible that would be relevant and current, we contacted campus and law enforcement officers throughout the country and requested that they share with us the knowledge they had gained and programs that they had developed to deal with so many of our mutual problems. The response to our request was overwhelming. In some instances, we have utilized material sent to us by them with very few changes and these are identified quite clearly throughout this book. In other instances, material provided was not used directly but it assisted us in developing a conceptual framework for organizing the book and including topics that we had not previously considered. We would now like to identify the individuals and their institutions for their generosity. This book would not have been possible without their support and cooperation.

D.E. Bowles, Chief, University of California, Berkeley, Berkeley, California; E.M. McEwen, Chief of Police, University of California, Davis, Davis, California; John J. Carpenter, Director of Public Safety, San Diego State University, San Diego, California; Douglas F. Tuttle, Director of Public Safety and Thomas Chisholm, Investigator, Crime Prevention Unit, University of Delaware, Newark, Delaware; William A. Tanner, Director of Public Safety and Sgt. Jim Bailey, Florida State University, Tallahassee, Florida; Paul Uravich, Director, and Lt. Robert Staehle, Division of Public Safety, University of South Florida, Tampa, Florida; Charles R. Riley, Safety Coordinator, Tallahassee Community College, Tallahassee, Florida; Frank Edwards, Fire Marshall, Asa T. Boynton, Director of Public Safety, and Pattie J. Williams, Corporal, Crime Prevention Unit, Public Safety Division, University of Georgia,

Athens, Georgia; Jack Vickery, Director of Campus Police, Georgia Institute of Technology, Atlanta, Georgia; Bill Byars, Director of Campus Security, Berry College, Mount Berry, Georgia; Dale F. Shaffer, Director of Public Safety, Northwestern University, Evanston, Illinois; Anne Glavin, Chief, Campus Police Department, Massachusetts Institute of Technology, Cambridge, Massachusetts; Eugene Sides, Director of Police, University of Maryland, College Park, Maryland; Robert C. Nielsen, Director of Public Safety, University of Maryland, Cantonsville, Maryland; Steven J. Murphy, Chief of Police, and Lt. Retha M. Jackson, Crime Prevention Coordinator, Towson State University, Towson, Maryland; Andrew P. McEntee, Support Services Commander, Department of Public Safety, Michigan State University, East Lansing, Michigan; Robert E. Sherman, Director and Sgt. Ned A. Comar, University Police, University of North Carolina at Chapel Hill, Chapel Hill, North Carolina; Jerry E. Hudson, Director of Public Safety, University of North Carolina, Charlotte, North Carolina; Paul J. Dumas, Director and Edward S. Godley, Lt., Public Safety Department, Duke University, Durham, North Carolina; James W. Cunningham, Director, Department of Public Safety, North Carolina State University, Raleigh, North Carolina; Joseph M. Johnson, Director of Police Service, University of North Carolina, Wilmington, North Carolina; Gail L. Gade, Chief, University Police, University of Nebraska, Lincoln, Nebraska; David A. Flanders, Director, and Paul H. Dean, Detective, Department of Public Safety, University of New Hampshire, Durham, New Hampshire; Robert F. Ochs, Assistant Vice-President for Public Safety, and Thomas E. Giordano, Lt., Police Department, State University of New Jersey, Rutgers, New Brunswick, New Jersey; Lee E. Griffin, Director, Jerry Denny, Investigator, and Bill Georger, Officer, Department of Public Safety, University of Buffalo, State University of New York, Buffalo, New York; Leslie A. Scoville, Director, Department of Campus Safety, Rochester Institute of Technology, Rochester, New York; David E. Stormer, Director, Department of University Safety, The Pennsylvania State University, University Park, Pennsylvania; George B. Stackhouse III, Director of Public Safety, The Citadel, Charleston, South Carolina; Saul Chaffin, Chief, Security and Safety Department, Vanderbilt University, Nashville, Tennessee; C. H. Cavender, Acting Director of Police, University of Texas, Austin, Texas; Max Clay, Director, Safety and Security Department, East Texas State University, Commerce, Texas; George Hess, Director and Malcolm Davis, Lt., University Police Department, University of Houston, Houston, Texas;

Robert W. Kelshaw, Chief of Police, and Paul Bringhurst, Crime Prevention Specialist, Brigham Young University, Provo, Utah; Arthur J. Sanders, Director and Blanche R.S. Cathcart, Crime Prevention Officer, Campus Police, George Mason University, Fairfax, Virginia; D.M. Dean, Director, Campus Police, Virginia Commonwealth University, Richmond, Virginia; Roger C. Serra, Assistant Chief of Police and Frank Moore, Sgt., Crime Prevention, University of Washington, Seattle, Washington; Donald L. Salyers, Director of Public Safety, Marshall University, Huntington, West Virginia.

We also wish to thank Magdalene Deutsch who typed this entire manuscript expertly and with good cheer despite our last-minute changes and pressure of deadlines. We also wish to thank Candace Christensen for all of her assistance in organizing the volumes of material that was received from the various colleges and universities throughout the country. She made what could have been a very difficult task much easier for us.

CONTENTS

COLLEGE CRIME PREVENTION AND PERSONAL SAFETY AWARENESS

Chapter 1

CRIME ON COLLEGE CAMPUSES

In this chapter, we will provide the reader with information regarding issues relative to crimes being committed on college campuses throughout the United States. Specifically, we will examine the need to study crimes on campus, review the extent to which crimes are being committed on campuses, perceptions of safety on colleges and universities, and examine who commits crimes on our campuses as well as who is typically victimized. There is little doubt that serious criminal acts have occurred at our institutions of higher learning and will continue to occur for the indefinite future. It is apparent that, regardless of the size, nature, or location of our campuses, criminal acts that occur within the collegiate setting will parallel those taking place in surrounding communities. In this chapter, we will examine some of the problems involved in attempting to make comparisons between campuses regarding their crime rates as well as the difficulties encountered in making comparisons between campus law enforcement agencies.

WHY STUDY CAMPUS CRIME?

College faculty, students, and administrators have become seriously concerned about the frequency and magnitude of crimes occurring within their campus settings. Likewise, parents of students now attending college are being made aware that college campuses are no longer sanctuaries, safe from the criminal activities which have traditionally plagued many of our local communities. The print and electronic media seem to be filled with headline stories such as the following:

"Nursing student raped—Sues university for failure to provide adequate security."
"Co-ed dragged from dorm at knife point and raped."
"Co-ed sexually molested and beaten in women's locker room."
"Rape-murder of co-ed in state-owned dorm."
"Co-ed raped after a date in parking lot adjacent to a dorm."
"Two students made victims of armed robbery/drug rip off in college residence hall."

The types of crimes mentioned in these headlines once occurred primarily in our large cities. Unfortunately, these types of serious incidents now occur too frequently on college campuses. Many colleges and universities are referred to by those who work within them as "cities within the city." Therefore, students, faculty, and administrative staff need to be made aware of their potential for victimization. They should also be provided with information that will be value to them in reducing the possibility of their becoming victims within their institutional settings. As a matter of fact, many colleges have been very active over the last fifteen years in the development and implementation of crime reduction programs. Today, programs which take proactive steps to prevent crimes on campuses are found throughout the country.

Campus administrators are also faced with potential liability issues when serious crimes occur on their campuses. The college administration and/or individual administrators may find themselves the target of third-party civil liability lawsuits. It is not unusual today for the victims of crimes or their families to assert that an institution did not take adequate steps to ensure the appropriate levels of security and safety as part of the fulfillment of their educational contracts. The American Council on Education, the National Association of Student Personnel Administrators, and the International Association of Campus Law Enforcement Administrators are examples of organizations that have been actively engaged in reviewing liability issues relative to campus security and crime.

HOW MUCH CRIME IS THERE?

Information regarding the actual volume of crimes which occur on college campuses throughout the United States is somewhat difficult to obtain. The officially recognized crime reporting program in the United States is called the Uniform Crime Report (UCR). The Federal Bureau of Investigation (FBI) serves as the national clearinghouse for the Uniform Crime Report. Eight crimes have been defined as the Index Crimes. The Index Crimes are frequently divided into two categories: violent crimes (murder, aggravated assault, forcible rape, and robbery) and crimes against property (burglary, larceny, motor vehicle theft, and arson).

In the UCR system, the crime rate of a given location is determined by the number of crimes committed per 100,000 population base. There are several limitations to the Uniform Crime Report system. They are as follows: contributions of crime data to the UCR are voluntary, many crimes which frequently occur throughout the country and on our campuses, such as drug-related crimes and vandalism, are not included in the crime rate, and if a series of crimes are committed in a single incident (a person is raped, their jewelry is stolen, and their house is burglarized), only the most serious crime (in this case the rape) is counted for UCR purposes.

In order for a crime to be officially counted it must first of all be reported to law enforcement authorities. There may be a wide variety of reasons as to why an individual may choose not to officially report a crime. Some of the reasons typically given include: belief that the police cannot apprehend the offender, feeling that the crime was too minor to report, fear that something may happen to them as a result of reporting the crime, and the belief that even if an individual is arrested that they will never be successfully prosecuted. The campus law enforcement agency must, likewise, have gained the respect of the community it serves in order for crimes to be reported to them.

There is another reason that an accurate description of crimes committed on our campuses is difficult to develop. Some institutions may prefer not to officially report crimes committed on their campus to the FBI Uniform Crime Report system. Some campus administrators may fear that their institutions will be unfavorably compared to others throughout the country if such information is made available. Other campus officials may believe that reporting crimes to an agency outside the institution would be counterproductive in terms of attracting new students and supporters to their programs. As a matter of fact, only approximately 10 percent of this nation's 3,000 colleges and universities report to the Uniform Crime Report on a regular basis.[1]

CRIME TRENDS/DEFINITIONS

Despite the limitations of the FBI's Uniform Crime Report program, it does provide a general reflection of crime trends across the country on our college campuses. The Uniform Crime Report compiled in 1988 provided the following statistical information regarding serious crimes on campus:[2]

Murder—7
Rapes—227
Armed robberies—506
Aggravated assaults—1,637

It would be useful at this point to list and briefly define some of the crimes which will be discussed further in this chapter as well as others which follow. These definitions are not necessarily the definitions which appear in the Uniform Crime Report or in state statutes, however, they should give the reader a brief explanation of the terms being used.

Rape—forced sexual intercourse
Armed robbery—theft involving a weapon or threat of violence
Burglary—illegal entry of a business/home/room to commit theft
Larceny—theft of property, money
Shoplifting—theft against a business by a patron
Internal theft—theft committed by an employee against the employer's business
Assault—act or threat of violence against a person
Vandalism—intentional act of property destruction
Drug-related crime—act which involves use, sale of an illegal drug or the relationship between an illegal drug and a criminal act
Arson—willful or malicious burning of property

While the Uniform Crime Report may never offer a completely accurate depiction of crimes committed on campuses throughout the country, other resources may be used in order to develop a clearer picture. For example, in 1987 Towson State University distributed a nationwide survey of campus crimes of violence to over 1,000 colleges and universities. Of those campuses returning the survey, numerous trends were revealed. Virtually all campuses responding had experienced physical and sexual assault, rape and vandalism. Furthermore, one-third of all survey respondents reported some increase in the types of violence identified on the survey instrument. Most institutions reported that greater than 50 percent of all types of violence were alcohol-related.[3] This type of survey information is very useful to supplement the UCR data.

PERCEPTION OF SAFETY

Despite the fact that serious crimes continue to occur on our campuses, many persons who study and work in these settings may be unaware of those criminal acts or may appear unconcerned about them being committed. For example, a *Newsweek* poll conducted of students throughout the United States posed as one of its questions: "How much do you worry about crime on or near your campus?" Forty-three percent of those responding answered "Not much" and 18 percent answered "Not at all." When this same survey asked the question: "What is the crime situation compared with when you started school?" only 17 percent students responded "worse." Only 23 percent of the students in this survey who lived on campus responded that they "took great care of their property."[4]

According to these surveys, many students are unaware of criminal acts on their campus or somewhat naive about the seriousness of them. The belief in many cases is that "It can't happen to me." However, if one examines the nationwide data on crimes that occur on and off our colleges, many campuses provide numerous opportunities for criminal acts to occur. In fact, the "It can't happen to me" syndrome may provide criminal opportunities which would not be present otherwise. Unfortunately, in some cases, it is only after a very serious criminal incident has occurred on campus that this perception is altered, at least temporarily.

TARGETS OF CAMPUS CRIME

It is a reality that many of the factors associated with criminal victimization throughout the country are present in most campus settings. For example, a significant proportion of most campus student populations is youthful. Nationwide victimization studies confirm that frequently it is people in their late teens and early twenties who are the victims of serious crimes. Another factor to be considered is the open nature of many campuses throughout the country. Many colleges and universities allow access to institutional property and buildings regardless of the time of day or night. This ease of access creates multiple opportunities for both crimes against persons and crimes against property to be committed. There is a delicate balance to be maintained between traditional academic access needs and providing reasonable security constraints to enhance the protection of the campus community. Some college administrations have been reluctant or unwilling to address this issue.

An issue related to the access question is the transient nature of most campus populations. Many students come and go to their respective colleges without developing a sense of community whereby people get to know one another and interact on a frequent basis. It is very difficult on many campuses to determine who the "strangers" are versus who is present for legitimate academic purposes. Likewise, there are many users of institutional facilities (e.g., gyms, libraries) who are not part of the academic community and may, indeed, be there to commit criminal acts.

A recent crime survey revealed that approximately one-fourth of this nation's households were touched by a crime of violence or theft.[5] Another report produced by the United States Department of Justice attempted to estimate the likelihood that a person will become a victim of crime during his or her lifetime. This report estimated that five out of six people would be victims of violent crime, either attempted or completed during their lifetime. This same study revealed that virtually everyone will be the victim of a personal theft at least once during his or her lifetime.[6] This information, of course, has some relevance to persons in college or university settings.

Thefts in particular are the most frequently committed crime on our college campuses today. Many thefts which occur on our campuses are strictly crimes of opportunity. That is, individuals have done little to protect or secure their property in the true sense of the word. Items which are frequently stolen from persons on campuses throughout the country include bicycles, petty cash, calculators, personal jewelry, and other objects which are readily obtainable and somewhat easy to conceal. Furthermore, if members of the campus community fail to lock their dormitory rooms or offices upon leaving them, there are additional opportunities created for would-be thieves.

As mentioned earlier, many people believe that our campuses today are small cities within cities. If one reviews a fairly typical campus regardless of its geographic setting (urban, suburban, or rural), you will find many of the targets of crime present—all of which have counterparts in their surrounding cities/communities. The following identifies specifically some of those frequent targets of crime and the types of crimes committed.

Community	*Campus*	*Crimes*
Motels, apartments	residence halls, Greek housing	assault, rape, theft, vandalism
Retail business	bookstores, textbook centers, sundry stores	robbery, shoplifting, burglary, internal theft

Banks	credit unions, registration centers, cashier's office	robbery, burglary, internal theft
Auditoriums, stadiums	concert halls, athletic facilities	robbery, assault, theft, vandalism
Convenience stores	campus 7–11 type stores	burglary, robbery, assault, rape
Fast-food restaurants	campus grills, McDonald's	burglary, robbery
Bars	campus pubs	assault, robbery
Parking lots	lots, garages	assault, rape, robbery
Hospitals	health center, infirmaries	burglary, internal theft, robbery
Parks	wooded/recreational areas	assault, rape, robbery

Each of these targets of crime create concerns for campus officials. Another way to review a campus for possible targets of crime is to consider the various classifications of persons who may be on campus on a daily basis. Students, faculty, staff members, administrative personnel, and visitors may all be potential victims at some point with varying degrees of probability. The potential for individual victimization may depend on a number of factors, for example: the extent to which those individuals are aware of prior crimes that have occurred on campus, safeguards which they may have taken, the actual length of time they are physically on the campus or in campus facilities, the time of day or night which they happen to be on campus and the actual kinds of activities which they are involved in while on campus. All of these factors may be associated with an individual's vulnerability.

Many campuses also sponsor events which invite large groups of non-affiliated persons to their settings. Examples might include on-campus special events such as concerts or athletic events, campus open houses, parents' day, etc. Each of these situations may create more opportunities for criminal victimization if crime prevention techniques are not practiced. Finally, it is safe to assume that regardless of the size of the institution, its particular geographic setting, or the nature of the student population served, property crimes and crimes of violence will continue to occur. Institutions as well as individuals have responsibilities to consider in that regard.

PROBLEMS WITH COMPARING CAMPUS CRIME RATES

There is a natural tendency on the part of many people to compare the actual number of crimes reported on a campus with the numbers reported on other colleges. It seems that when an institution makes its annual report regarding the number of crimes reported, many individuals quickly ask for comparison figures related to other institutions within their state or, in some cases, other institutions throughout the United States. While this comparison may be tempting for some administrators or members of the media, the results are usually not very persuasive when one examines the issues more comprehensively.

CAMPUS VARIATIONS

There is, in fact, a wide variation in the crime rate among institutions throughout our country. These variations, which are well beyond the control of the campus law enforcement agency, may impact not only the campus crime rate but other campus security issues. In the remainder of this section, we shall attempt to discuss some of the variables which not only affect crime rates on individual campuses but make more difficult the comparison of crime rate between campuses.

For example, one of the first variables often examined for comparison purposes is the size of the student enrollment. While two institutions may have approximately the same number of students, a further question one should ask relates to the actual percentage of students who are full-time residents of the campus versus those who are commuters. The ratio of day versus night students is also an appropriate question to consider when making comparisons. Another factor to consider is the size of the average daily on-campus population. This figure will include the number of faculty present, the number of students present, as well as the approximate number of visitors or non-affiliated persons who are on campus on a daily basis. Some campuses, for example, may have a fairly small student enrollment but have rather large faculty-to-student ratios. Other campuses may have significant community outreach programs, which encourage large numbers of non-affiliated personnel to visit the campus on a daily or weekly basis. These variations can greatly affect the average daily population on campus and thus, in turn, have an impact on potential criminal opportunities.

Another consideration is the actual size or geographic acreage of the campuses being compared. Some campuses are very large in land mass, while others are located on a few city blocks or maybe within a few high-rise buildings. The number of actual buildings which are located on the campus site can be a significant factor regarding the overall security of the campus and the need for specialized forms of protection. Multiple buildings spread out over a large geographic area can create their own unique security problems. Another issue relates to the types of equipment in the campus buildings. For example, are the rooms in the buildings used primarily for lectures, or do they contain large quantities of expensive electronic equipment which is fairly portable and may require additional security measures to prevent thefts? Decisions about the method of deploying campus law enforcement personnel, the use of alarms, and the installation of surveillance cameras are examples of factors which must be considered as a result of these variations among campuses.

The actual location of the campuses will effect their crime rate. For example, is the campus located in a downtown inner-city area which has a significant crime rate in and of itself, or is the campus located in a rural or suburban site with a relatively lower crime rate? It is important to consider the size of the town or city in which the campus may be located or adjacent to. If the campus is located in a "suburban" area but is adjacent to a large city which itself has a high crime rate, in all likelihood there will be a spillover effect relative to the frequency and types of crimes occurring on the campus. Very few criminals make a distinction between where a city's boundary stops and a campuses' begins. It is also important to note the nature and variety of other facilities found around the campus area regardless of the actual location of the campus itself. For example, campuses located in close proximity to large shopping malls may well experience crimes similar to those being committed at the malls themselves. If a shopping mall near a college is plagued by cars being burglarized in the parking lots, similar patterns of thefts from on-campus vehicles frequently develop.

Whether the college is a privately owned and operated institution or whether it is publicly funded one may be a factor to consider before making any comparison of crime rates or campus security related issues. Private institutions, for example, can generally be more restrictive regarding non-affiliates accessing their campus property on a 24-hour basis. Most public institutions are considered to be open to virtually all members of the public, with only certain truly restricted areas. Also, as a general rule, campus law enforcement officers at public institutions are more likely than their private counterparts to have arrest authority and to practice "traditional" policing responsibilities similar to municipal agencies.

Before making comparisons between the level of campus security or crime rates between institutions, one should also consider the types of "specialized" facilities housed on campus grounds and their anticipated usage. For example, some campuses have very large football stadiums which may attract in excess of 50,000 people on a given Saturday afternoon. Specialized security and traffic needs will be present on the campus during the weekend of those football games that are not normally in existence the remainder of the year. During these large-scale sporting events, campuses typically experience a significant increase in alcohol-related infractions, assaults, and property crimes committed in and around the stadiums.

Many campuses that do not have large football stadiums have constructed arenas for the purpose of hosting basketball games, concerts, and other fairly large spectator events. While the overall number of visitors in attendance at a specific event may not compare with the 50,000 spectators in a football stadium, they will in all likelihood have some impact on the level of campus security and the potential for additional crimes to be committed on the respective campus. If alcohol and drug use is fairly prevalent at the event (as we see in many concert settings), campus law enforcement officials may have, on a short-term basis, an increased level of criminal activity ranging from the very minor to the very serious in nature. Simply stated, the types of specialized facilities on a respective campus and their particular usage are important factors to consider before making any comparison between campuses relative to their crime rates.

A major variable to consider when comparing the relative level of campus security among institutions is the actual number of full-time resident students as compared with the overall enrollment figures. Many campuses throughout the country that have large on-campus residential populations have a significantly higher rate of reported crimes when compared to other campuses. For example, two campuses when compared may have an equal enrollment of 10,000 students. However, one campus may actually have 7,000 of the 10,000 students living on campus 24 hours a day in residence halls. The second campus may only have 3,000 students actually living in the residence hall population on campus.

As a general rule, the campus with the larger number of on-campus students residing 24 hours a day will have a higher rate of reported crimes when compared to a campus with fewer full-time residents. The presence of Greek (fraternity and/or sorority) housing may be a factor to consider when reviewing the nature and frequency of criminal activity on a college campus. This does not mean to imply that students who join Greek organizations are responsible for a disproportionate number of criminal acts on our college campuses. However, one cannot ignore the official reports and media statements regarding serious alcohol-related incidents, injuries, assaults, vandalism, and other serious acts which have been directly associated with members of Greek organizations throughout the country.

PROBLEMS WITH COMPARING CAMPUS LAW ENFORCEMENT AGENCIES

In addition to comparing the crime rates between institutions, some individuals suggest that it is appropriate to likewise compare the campus law enforcement departments at respective institutions. Similar to comparing campus crime rates, there are numerous factors to consider before making a valid comparison of one campus law enforcement agency to another. A recent survey of campus law enforcement agencies underscores the wide-scale variation that is present throughout the country. When Stormer surveyed members of the International Association of Campus Law Enforcement Administrators in 1986, the information compiled revealed many differences among campus law enforcement agencies.[7] Of those responding, approximately 67 percent identified campus departments themselves as representing public institutions and 33 percent private institutions. The full-time equivalent student enrollments of those responding were as follows: more than 20,000 students, 12 percent; 10 to 20,000 students, 20 percent; less than 10,000 students, 53 percent; not specifying, 12 percent. The survey also revealed that the number of students per officer increased as the size of the institution increased. This study found wide diversity relative to campus law enforcement organizational size, manner in which the campus law enforcement agencies are constituted, as well as functions performed by the law enforcement organizations. Some of the non-police functions which are also provided by the campus law enforcement agencies are listed below. The survey indicated that private campus law enforcement agencies tended to provide a wider variety of the non-police functions than did their public counterparts.

Function	Private (%)	Public (%)
Security	97.6	96.2
Parking administration	82.7	72.9
Parking 24-hour enforcement	84.6	87.3
Environmental health and safety	56.1	49.4
Fire prevention	79.7	59.4
Fire suppression	33.3	24.3
Key control	48.8	38.2
Key shop	17.1	15.9
Transportation	16.3	15.9
Telephone switchboard	37.4	28.3

This list reflects the wide variety of functions served by campus law enforcement agencies throughout the country in varying degrees. Also noted in the study was the fact that public institutions were most likely to maintain campus law enforcement agencies which had vested arrest authority. This arrest authority also varied with the size of the institution. The larger institutions (whether they were public or private in nature) frequently had vested arrest powers as well. Arrest authority was generally established by either a state law or a local law.

In addition to some of the variations which were highlighted above, campus law enforcement agencies throughout the country may differ significantly in terms of their personnel hiring standards or training requirements. For example, some campus law enforcement agencies may require applicants to have achieved some college credit before applying and to have some prior law enforcement experience. Other campuses may require no college but a minimal level of prior law enforcement experience. The training which a campus law enforcement officer is required to obtain may also vary from institution to institution. Many agencies throughout the country now require a mandatory level of preservice training. However, there may be significant differences between the number of hours required and the actual curriculum of the training itself. Requiring new officers to complete a field training program after they have completed their mandatory preservice training is an accepted practice throughout the country today. Once again, however, differences exist relating to the degree of sophistication and commitment to this type of training. Frequently, the professional background, level of higher education, and prior training of the chief of the campus law enforcement agency is a significant factor in determining the hiring and training standards for an individual department. Throughout the country, there are many examples of proactive, progressive campus law enforcement administrators as well as those who are more reactive in their approach and traditional in their management philosophies. These fundamental differences in management approach contribute to the difficulty encountered in attempting to make valid comparisons between campus law enforcement departments.

SUGGESTED SECURITY QUESTIONS

1. Do students, faculty, staff, and non-affiliates expect to be safe/secure within your campus setting?
2. What are the expectations of parents of students regarding security?
3. What are the expectations of the Board of Trustees and administrators of the campus regarding security?
4. Have serious criminal incidents been committed on campuses similar to yours?
5. Have serious criminal incidents been committed on your campus?
6. Does the campus exercise reasonable security measures in attempting to reduce criminal opportunities?
7. Do the campus administrators or law enforcement personnel conduct their own security audit and correct any deficiencies that are found?
8. Is information regarding security and safety issues routinely made available to students, faculty, and staff?
9. Is the campus administration generally familiar with campus security/liability issues?
10. Has the campus administration identified desirable and important characteristics in the selection of new campus law enforcement officers?
11. In seeking to identify those characteristics, have campus community needs been assessed?
12. Are staff, faculty, and students involved in the campus law enforcement officer selection process?
13. Does the chief of the campus law enforcement department express and operationalize values which are shared by the campus administration?

14. What level of preservice training is given to new campus law enforcement officers?
15. Are both technical and people skills included in the training given to the campus law enforcement officers?
16. Does the preservice training given to campus law enforcement officers relate to the jobs which they will actually be performing?
17. Does the campus law enforcement department use a field training program for officers who have recently graduated from a training academy?
18. Does the campus law enforcement department have regularly scheduled in-service training for its officers?
19. Are campus-oriented topics included in the campus law enforcement officer in-service training programs?
20. Do the campus law enforcement departmental first-line supervisors become actively involved in in-service training?

ENDNOTES

1. *Uniform Crime Report* for 1985, U.S. Department of Justice (U.S. Government Printing Office, Washington, D.C., 1985), pp. 110–117.
2. UCR 1988, pp. 110–117.
3. "Campus Violence Survey" (unpublished compilation, Office of Student Services, Towson State University, 1987).
4. *Newsweek on Campus,* February, 1986, p. 10.
5. Rand, M.R. "Households Touched by Crime," 1986. Washington, D.C.: U.S. Department of Justice, Bureau of Justice Statistics, 1987.
6. Koppel, H. "Lifetime Likelihood of Victimization." Washington, D.C.: U.S. Department of Justice, Bureau of Justice Statistics, 1987.
7. Patterson, Jr., R.M. "University Law Enforcement Survey Part I and Part II," *Campus Law Enforcement Journal* (May–June 1987), pp. 42–44, and *Campus Law Enforcement Journal* (July–August, 1987), pp. 38–40.

Chapter 2

DEVELOPING A CAMPUS-WIDE
APPROACH TO CRIME PREVENTION

Many people believe that preventing crime on a college campus is the sole responsibility of the campus law enforcement agency. While the campus law enforcement agency is, of course, the primary department responsible for providing a safe, secure atmosphere on any college campus, we would argue that in order for crime prevention to be successful, a more comprehensive campus-wide approach must be taken.

Similar to their municipal counterparts, the campus law enforcement agency is too often called into a situation after the crime has occurred. This approach is defined as a reactive strategy to policing and is one which has not proven to be successful. Many campus law enforcement agencies across the country have initiated proactive crime prevention programs which serve to educate their communities and reduce opportunities for crimes to occur within their campus setting. In spite of the efforts of progressive campus law enforcement authorities, serious crimes still occur on many campuses and, in some cases, with a significant degree of frequency. The campus law enforcement department needs the cooperation of many other departments and campus personnel in order to successfully deal with the crime problem.

In this chapter, we will provide the rationale for involving other campus departments and constituents in order to develop a campus-wide approach to crime prevention. We will also discuss comprehensive policy issues which must be reviewed with security in mind.

THE ROLE OF SENIOR CAMPUS ADMINISTRATORS IN SECURITY

Chancellors, presidents, vice-presidents and other senior administrators at higher education institutions are very aware of the serious crimes being committed within their boundaries. Persons in these positions must provide leadership and policy guidance relating to security issues. Executives at this level must assume responsibility for developing security policies for their respective colleges and provide needed resources for their accomplishment. Many administrators now recognize that while the campus law enforcement department is an extremely important component of the overall security of the institution, it is by no means the only one. In many institutions, it has been found effective to implement a "team-oriented" approach to security-related problems.

Senior-level administrators have become increasingly aware that if they fail to provide an adequate level of security on their campus, they may be subjecting their institution and themselves personally to third-party civil liability lawsuits. That is to say, crime victims or their families may assert that the institution and top officials did not take steps necessary to ensure the appropriate level of security. Two case summaries below illustrate this point:

In 1980, a jury awarded a woman law student $215,000 as a result of a suit that she brought against the Hastings Law Center in California. The state of California and the Governing Board of Regents for the University were listed in the lawsuit. The former law student had been sexually assaulted in a women's restroom at the Hastings Law Center at the University of California (*Siciliano* v. *State*).

The Massachusetts Supreme Court made a $20,000 award to a student who had been raped on the Pine Manor College campus. In 1983, this court found against the college and its Vice-President for Operations (*Mullins* v. *Pine Manor College*).

Cases such as these illustrate that it is only prudent that university officials do all that they can to ensure that there is a properly coordinated and comprehensive approach to campus security and crime prevention among the units and departments within the institution. It is essential that appropriate administrative units take a proactive approach regarding safety and security on campus. This would help place all parties in a more defensible position regarding future liability suits brought against them. The president, provost, the chief student affairs officer, the administrative vice-president, as well as the legal counsel's office each have a role to play in this regard. The following are among the most important security topics to be reviewed by administrators at higher educational institutions.

DEFINING THE ROLE OF
CAMPUS LAW ENFORCEMENT DEPARTMENTS

A critical decision which must be made by the top administrators of the institution regards the appropriate role of the campus law enforcement agency. At some institutions, and in some locations, it is a necessity that the campus law enforcement agency have sworn arrest authority and operate in many ways similar to their local police counterparts. At other institutions, it may be more appropriate for the campus law enforcement agency not to have arrest authority and to function in ways similar to traditional security departments. A third model found to be very popular at many institutions is the comprehensive department which includes both a "sworn" campus police component which has full arrest authority and a "non-sworn" component which provides many security functions which do not require a certified police officer.

The role chosen by the institution's leadership for its campus law enforcement department should be clearly defined for both the campus community and the city or town in which the campus is located. Regardless of the specific duties of campus law enforcement personnel, there should be a close working relationship between the campus law enforcement agency and the local police department which services the surrounding community. A clear understanding of which department (campus or local police) is responsible for which kinds of activities on campus is very important. For example, will the campus law enforcement department be solely responsible for vehiclar traffic control at large-scale on-campus special events (e.g., rock concerts, athletic events) or will the local police also play a role? If a serious crime such as a murder or rape occurs on campus, will the local police be called for assistance and at what point? The occurrence of natural disasters such as floods or tornadoes will probably necessitate a significant level of interaction between campus law enforcement personnel and local police authorities. This understanding should be worked out well in advance before an emergency occurs on campus. Many campuses and local police departments have clearly defined "mutual aid agreements" which help to ensure good cooperation in critical situations. Communication between the two departments should be frequent at both the formal and informal level.

The campus executive management team must ensure that the its law enforcement agency has professional leadership. The prior training, professional experience, and level of higher education attained by the chief of the campus law enforcement agency are a reflection of the institution's value structure. Therefore, considerable time and effort should be taken in the selection of a campus law enforcement chief. Once a chief is hired, the institution's executive leadership must ensure that professional hiring and training standards are adopted within the campus law enforcement agency. Top administrators furthermore should ensure that the resources are available to help the chief achieve these professional standards and goals. Further, they should also require that the campus law enforcement agency, above all else, have a strong service orientation that displays a humanistic, democratic approach to all individuals with whom they have contact.

OPEN INFORMATION POLICY

For a variety of reasons, some executives at institutions of higher education have traditionally chosen not to make public serious criminal acts which have occurred on their campuses. The belief often was that to do so would create a bad image for the institution and, in fact, turn away potential students and other resources. In the decades of the eighties and nineties, this approach to the management of information regarding serious criminal incidents will in all likelihood become less desirable or possible. One reason for this is that serious incidents will continue to occur on our nation's college campuses regardless of the level of security provided. In addition, as stated earlier, civil liability lawsuits against institutions for failing to provide adequate security will, in all likelihood, become more popular and more publicized.

One of the issues examined frequently in these lawsuits is whether or not the institution was aware of serious incidents occurring on and around the campus and was this information shared with the campus community for its own self-protection? A lack of affirmative responses to these questions on the part of an institution will not only be embarrassing but could also quite costly in terms of dollars lost in a lawsuit.

Campus executives should establish policies wherein criminal activity occurring on and around campus is periodically reviewed and relayed to the campus community. Many campuses now have very active crime prevention/public education programs. These programs involve the release of information to campus and local newspapers regarding criminal acts and prevention measures. Often, brochures are developed which highlight steps people can take to reduce their chances of being victimized.

Public information/awareness lectures are frequently held by campus law enforcement officials. Top campus administrators should encourage crime prevention information to be shared at orientation sessions, student meetings, and other appropriate forums.

Some campus administrators have also allowed campus law enforcement officials to serve as guest lecturers in academic classes. This provides valuable information to students regarding criminal acts and prevention, as well as establishing a positive means of interaction and communication between the student body and campus law enforcement officials. These same kinds of educational programs need to be encouraged and made available to campus staff and faculty. Suggested means for initiating these public education programs will be described in a later chapter.

ACCESS TO CAMPUS BUILDINGS

Another issue which relates directly to the overall level of security on a campus is access to buildings. Decisions must be made regarding when buildings should be open on a general basis and when they may be reasonably restricted. Some buildings such as libraries or student centers may need a wide degree of open access. Other facilities which store valuable, highly portable equipment (e.g., personal computers) should have a more restrictive-access policy. The decision as to how to appropriately balance traditional academic freedom with maintaining the security/integrity of buildings and equipment is not an easy one to make. There needs to be open dialogue among faculty, students, and administrators on this topic in an attempt to reach consensus.

Restricting persons not affiliated with the college from on-campus facilities is also an issue which needs to be addressed. Reasonable access should be allowed but not to the extent that it interferes with the normal education process. Freedom of speech, assembly, and other constitutional issues must be examined thoroughly. Campus executives have a duty to uphold the Constitution but also have a responsibility to establish reasonable security to enhance the educational mission and to provide protection to the overall community. Sufficient case law has been developed in this area. Assistance from the campus legal advisor's office should be sought regarding restriction of access, trespass authority, and other related topics. Furthermore, all departments within the campus setting and members of the campus community should be informed as to these policies once they are established.

SCHEDULING ACADEMIC CLASSES AND EMPLOYEE WORK HOURS

Traditionally, little thought has been given regarding the relationship between security and where and when classes should be held on campus. Frequently, their decisions are made upon past practices and instructor preference. While these may be valid reasons for establishing class schedules and locations, security concerns should also be taken into consideration. For example, factors such as the level of pedestrian and vehicular traffic in and around a campus building should be considered when a determination is made regarding evening classes. Relative isolation may provide the opportunity for serious criminal acts to occur. Likewise, the more isolated the campus classroom setting, the more difficult it is for the campus law enforcement agency to adequately provide patrol and other security services. The amount of parking and level of lighting available adjacent to classroom buildings should be considered when scheduling evening classes. Some institutions have considered, and eventually instituted, policies which require evening classes to be taught on central campus locations which have a higher volume of people in and around the area.

Many campus employees frequently work after 5:00 P.M. and on the weekends in their offices. This, too, can provide an opportunity for criminal acts to occur if a staff member is working alone or is an isolated part of the campus. While it may be impossible to preclude these work situations from occurring, some additional security measures should be taken when they are necessary. For example, departmental managers can require that at least two persons stay in a building if after-hours work becomes necessary. If this is not possible, all exterior doors to the building as well as exterior office doors should be secured when all workers vacate the building. The campus law enforcement agency should be advised when there is someone working alone in the building after hours or on the weekend. A request for periodic security checks by campus law enforcement agency can also be made a standard operating practice when staff or faculty are working in isolation.

ADMINISTRATIVE PREPARATION
FOR SERIOUS CAMPUS INCIDENTS

It is essential that the executive leadership in the institution be prepared for the eventuality of a serious criminal incident occurring on their campus. One researcher recommends that campus administrators address a number of specific issues in order to successfully deal with a campus tragedy. There should first and foremost be a campus emergency operations plan which identifies specific emergencies, resources available, and delineates who is responsible for which activities during and after such an event. Specifically, the role of student affairs officials, administrative services, campus legal counsel, and the campus law enforcement agency should be identified in advance. On-call procedures should be established on a 24-hour basis, with the campus law enforcement agency serving as the notifying department. Campus personnel should be assigned in advance the responsibility to notify next of kin in the case of the death of a student or other person on campus. A single media spokesperson should be identified to handle all news releases and similar requests. Care should be taken to ensure that quality reports are written regarding all facets of the incident itself. And, finally, rumor control mechanisms should be established during and after any major campus incident.[1]

The authors saw firsthand the importance of establishing clear communications and a mechanism for rumor control after the brutal murder and rape of a secretary at their university. Immediately following this tragic event, the campus police department established a campus-wide series of briefing sessions for all interested persons. Over a thousand university community members attended these sessions over a three-day period. This open and honest response to one of the most serious events which had ever occurred on the campus was instrumental in reducing rumors about the incident. The services of professional counselors were also made available to the campus personnel in order to assist those who needed help in dealing with their grief and trauma.

THE ROLE OF THE CAMPUS LEGAL ADVISOR

The campus legal advisor plays a very important role in security issues on our college campuses. In this decade, most campuses have either employed an attorney as part of the administrative staff of the college or have retained the services of a legal advisor on a year-round basis. Given the level of potential litigation facing our colleges today, the importance of the legal advisor's office has increased enormously.

One important function served by the legal advisor is to review legal requirements regarding the campus law enforcement department. For example, issues such as the authority of the campus law enforcement agency, its geographic jurisdiction, mandated selection requirements, and training standards are all important factors for the campus legal office to be familiar with. The legal advisor's office should assist the campus law enforcement agency in developing policies and procedures which accurately reflect requirements such as those mentioned in preceding examples. The legal advisor should also assist the campus law enforcement department in developing policies which address "high-risk" liability areas. The operation of emergency vehicles, use of force, and arrest techniques would all be considered tasks performed by campus law enforcement officers which could create high-risk liability potential if proper policies were not developed and followed.

The campus legal advisor can be of assistance in the development of policies regarding public access to campus facilities. The legal advisor can provide important input before final campus access policies are instituted. The legal advisor will incorporate constitutional protections in the policy which is eventually developed for the campus. Likewise, the legal advisor will ensure that the campus policies are consistent with state statutory requirements or local ordinances.

Many campuses have developed public information policies which provide guidelines for the release of information to members of the public and media. The campus legal advisor should review all policies relating to the release of public information to ensure consistency with federal and/or state statutory requirements. This is a very important issue, as it relates to crimes committed on the campus, the public release of names of victims or witnesses, and the sharing of information regarding the formal arrest of students.

As mentioned earlier in this chapter, some campus administrations have been reluctant to release information concerning crimes committed at their institutions. At the present time, many states are considering the enactment of legislation which requires colleges and universities to provide parents and potential students accurate information regarding the rate of crime and other security issues on campus. The state of Pennsylvania was the forerunner in implementing this type of legislation. The legislation in Pennsylvania was lobbied for by the parents of Jeanne

Cleary, a student who was murdered on the campus of Lehigh University in 1986. This law in Pennsylvania may be the future model that other states eventually emulate. The campus legal advisor will play a significant role in this area of public information.

In the event a campus has a liability suit brought against it, one of the decisions the campus legal advisor may have to face is whether or not to obtain an expert witness. If a decision is made to hire the services of an expert witness in the campus security field, another decision must be then be reached as to which expert to retain for the provision of those services. The selection of a proper security expert may mean the difference between winning or losing a case which, of course, has serious financial and public relations implications for the college or university.

In making the selection of a security expert, the legal advisor should consider evaluating the potential security expert in the following areas: prior experience, specialized training completed, education level, writing skills, and courtroom experience.[2] For example, experts who possess an advanced degree in a field such as criminal justice, prior campus law enforcement-related experience, specialized law enforcement/security training, and a positive track record as a courtroom witness would be excellent candidates to consider to represent the college. The expert can provide excellent service in reviewing case materials and offering advice even if a decision is made to settle a case out of court.

INVOLVING CAMPUS DEPARTMENTS
IN CRIME PREVENTION EFFORTS

In this section of the chapter, we will discuss the need for and advantages of involving many campus departments in the comprehensive crime prevention efforts. In identifying the individual departments, we will review their general responsibilities, list the types of crimes which they might play a role in reducing, and describe what steps they might take to become crime prevention oriented. One researcher has suggested that an institution-wide crime prevention program should include realistic goals.[3] They are listed as follows:

1. identify crime problems and potential criminal activity
2. educate the campus community to the reality of future crime on campus
3. make all campus community members aware of the responsibility in becoming involved to reduce the opportunities for crime

4. develop a comprehensive crime prevention plan involving all constituencies within the campus community
5. develop and implement specifically targeted crime prevention programs

The Campus Law Enforcement Department

The mission of the campus law enforcement department is to provide those services necessary to help ensure a safe, secure atmosphere which is conducive to the attainment of educational objectives of the institution. The campus law enforcement agency is usually involved in functions such as patrol, investigation, traffic control, and public education programs which are designed to reduce the opportunity for crime and traffic accidents to occur. The campus law enforcement agency has an obvious role to play in all crimes or other serious incidents which occur on the campus. The operating philosophy of the campus law enforcement department is critical to the successful attainment of crime prevention goals. In the future, departments that are service oriented and have a crime prevention operational philosophy will be among the more successful.

The selection of personnel who share those operating philosophies and providing them with adequate training once hired are two elements critical to the success of a campus law enforcement agency. Some of the selection techniques used by model campus law enforcement agencies include the following: individual applicant interviews by a key member of the campus law enforcement agency staff, oral review boards which are comprised of members of the campus law enforcement department, faculty, staff, and students, thorough background investigations on all applicants considered for hiring, use of psychological screening tests and interviews to help determine emotional suitability of applicants, extensive physical examination, and screening for illegal drugs. The proper use of selection techniques will greatly enhance the department's efforts. It should also be stated that it is very important that the campus law enforcement department select personnel who share the crime prevention, community-oriented philosophy as opposed to a rigid "enforcement of the law approach."

Adequate training of the personnel selected to be campus law enforcement officers is another essential ingredient to the success of the department. The community-oriented values should be reinforced in addition to ensuring training in the attainment of necessary skills. The training should relate specifically to the functions to be performed by the campus law enforcement officer and be consistent with the campus administration's role expectations. If statutory training requirements are in existence, they must be met. Training must also be kept current in order to provide officers with the appropriate resources to do their job.

Physical Plant Department

Physical plant departments have the responsibility to maintain and improve campus facilities. On many campuses, the physical plant department will be responsible for building maintenance, utilities, custodial services, grounds maintenance, and transportation. On some campuses, the physical plant department also has responsibility for postal services, telecommunications, and the key shop.

Due to the wide variety of functions served by the physical plant department, it may play an important role in crime prevention by reducing the potential for burglaries, assaults, thefts, parking lot thefts and vandalism. For example, the adequacy of lighting is an important factor to consider when reviewing the opportunities for crimes to occur. The physical plant department can help to determine the adequacy of lighting and make appropriate alterations as necessary. A campus lighting survey should be conducted periodically to review both internal and external campus lighting needs. The level of lighting in campus parking lots, on sidewalks, on pedestrian pathways, and outside of building or dormitory entries needs to be periodically reviewed with an eye toward security. It is important to review the level of lighting in stairwells and hallways within buildings and dormitories. In addition to determining where new lighting might be needed, it is also important that the institution have a system wherein lights that have burned out are replaced in a timely fashion with proper documentation made. While it is difficult to measure the crimes which may be prevented by adequate lighting, a sufficient level of lighting on a campus helps to reinforce the perception of a safe and secure atmosphere.

Grounds maintenance is also an important function served by the physical plant department. Campuses usually spend a significant amount of time, effort, and money ensuring the adequate maintenance of hedges, shrubs, and other greenery on the campus site. This is usually done in order to enhance the attractiveness of the overall physical facility itself. However, in addition to aiding in the beautification of a campus, a proactive grounds-keeping service may also play a role in the reduction of criminal opportunities.

Shrubs and trees in and around building entries and windows to the buildings should be properly maintained so as not to provide a place of concealment for would-be assailants or burglars. Trees should not be allowed to grow to the extent that they block out a street light which may be adjacent to buildings and pathways. Periodic grounds-keeping surveys should be conducted with the reduction of potential criminal opportunities as one of the goals. As with the lighting surveys and alterations, the grounds-keeping survey and subsequent corrective actions should be properly documented.

On many campuses, the physical plant department is also responsible for the key shop. This often includes the issuance of new keys, the collection of keys from personnel once they terminate from campus employment, the keying or rekeying of all campus buildings and facilities, and the appropriate record keeping regarding these functions. Each of these tasks should be subject to very specific guidelines in the form of policy statements. Stiff financial penalties should be imposed against persons losing campus keys, and periodic inventories of keys should be conducted. If the campus uses a master key system, those keys should be issued only to persons having an absolute requirement to have them.

If the physical plant department is involved in the renovation of campus offices or other facilities, this is an ideal opportunity to employ proactive crime prevention techniques. During the planning of a building renovation project, it is helpful to review what steps might be taken to provide for additional security before the actual labor begins. For example, if a room is to be remodeled in such a way as to eventually house numerous personal computers, it is relatively easy and less expensive to install security hardware during the renovation process as opposed to doing so after the remodeling is completed. Too frequently, the security of a facility or office area which is undergoing renovation is only thought of after the personnel reoccupy the facility. By that time, it is often too late and too expensive to add additional elements of security. Major renovation projects on a campus should be coordinated between the physical plant and campus law enforcement department.

Many physical plant departments are in charge of campus transportation or the vehicle motor pool operation. This is also an opportunity for the physical plant department to become involved in campus crime prevention. For example, vehicles and other expensive equipment which are maintained in a motor pool area should be carefully inventoried and accounted for on a daily basis. Up-to-date records should be maintained as to vehicle usage and the identity of the last party responsible for the security of same. Tight control should be maintained over the keys to all vehicles, both day and night.

If a vehicle compound is maintained, it is recommended that it be properly fenced, well-lit, and be equipped with an alarm that is connected to the campus law enforcement department. Accurate records of gasoline dispensed at the motor pool should be kept. Vehicle maintenance equipment should be maintained under lock and key after normal working hours, with any exceptions completely documented. No one should be allowed to work in the motor pool area after normal business hours unless permission is granted and proper supervision is available.

The physical plant department and its personnel can be of great assistance in the campus-wide prevention effort in at least one other way. That is, physical plant personnel can serve as "eyes and ears" for the crime prevention program and contact the campus law enforcement department should they see or hear suspicious activity. Physical plant personnel are usually dispersed throughout the institution both within and outside of building facilities. In many cases, they serve the campus on a 24-hour-a-day basis and on weekends. They are in an ideal position to take an active role in crime prevention. On some campuses, physical plant vehicles are equipped with citizen band radios which are linked to the campus law enforcement department radio dispatcher. Reports of crimes or suspicious activities can then be radioed to the campus law enforcement dispatcher. Members of the physical plant department are very familiar with the campus facilities and grounds and, therefore, are in an excellent position to recommend changes that will enhance the overall security of the institution. Financial rewards or other forms of recognition could be given to members of physical plant departments who had actively participated in campus crime reduction efforts.

Facilities Planning Department

On many campuses, it is the responsibility of the facilities planning department to enhance the future physical environment of the institution. This department plans, designs and administers construction of new buildings and facilities for the campus. Planning, architecture, and engineering are among the services often provided. A facilities planning department may play a role in the campus crime prevention efforts regarding crimes such as sexual assaults, armed robbery, theft, and burglary.

During the last two decades, architectural planners and criminal justice practitioners have begun working together in an effort to reduce the opportunities for criminal acts through the adequate, preplanning and designing of the physical environments of new facilities, neighborhoods, and communities. In some cities, police departments and urban planners jointly review the security needs of new facilities and public works projects. This same working relationship has developed on campuses between the facilities planning department and the campus law enforcement agency. For example, internal and external building security, lighting, pedestrian walkway design, parking lot layout, and street configurations can all be examined from a security standpoint prior to new facility construction commencing.

These factors can be reviewed by the facilities planning department and the campus law enforcement department in order to enhance the security of the new building during the design stage. The physical security of all campus facilities should be constantly monitored and evaluated with recommendations for change being made as needed. This is a process which most architects and facility planning personnel do automatically for fire safety standpoint but have traditionally been lacking for security needs.

Environmental Health And Safety Department

The major responsibilities of an environmental health and safety department are to minimize injuries to people and reduce potential health hazards. Frequently, the campus safety department is responsible for biological, chemical, fire, and radiation safety programs on campus. On many campuses, the safety department of safety officer are part of the campus law enforcement agency. While the safety department may not be specifically charged with responsibilities in crime prevention, they share a common responsibility with the law enforcement department to reduce hazards on campus. Also, as is the case with personnel in the physical plant department, the safety department has personnel working throughout the campus grounds and facilities and they are in an ideal position to either identify suspicious activity or to report potential opportunities for crime to the campus law enforcement department.

On some campuses, the safety department also serves as a clearinghouse for campus-wide fire alarm systems. Again, there is a parallel, if not somewhat of an overlap, with the campus law enforcement department who may have complete or shared responsibility regarding security alarm installation, hardware, and maintenance. Shared training experiences between the campus law enforcement department and safety department can also be very valuable in the overall provision of safety and security services on the campus.

Procurement Department

At many campus locations, the procurement department offers a variety of services which may include the following: purchasing, receiving, print shop, and scientific supply store. Good security practices by the procurement department will assist the campus in its crime prevention efforts, particularly as it relates to the crimes of burglary and larceny. There are an ample number of targets for these property crimes which typically are part of a procurement department's responsibility. For example, many purchasing departments serve as the central receiving area for goods to be redelivered to various units within the campus. Surplus property may also be maintained at the purchasing department warehouse or compound areas.

Some examples of practices which have been used by procurement departments in an effort to reduce criminal opportunities in the property storage area and aid in the overall crime prevention effort include the following:

1. Require a single checkpoint or entrance/exit to the main equipment storage area.
2. Always ensure that an adequate number of purchasing staff are available and on-site during normal business hours.
3. High-risk items such as cameras, calculators, cassette tapes, VCR monitors, and so forth should be secured in rooms or locked cabinets out of the sight of the general population.
4. Limit the number of access keys to the purchasing warehouse facilities.
5. Assign a staff member to check cabinets, doors, and windows at the end of each normal workday.
6. Place high-risk items and equipment away from existing doors or windows.
7. Ensure adequate lighting at compound and warehouse entrances as well as near window areas.
8. Place fire exit alarms on doors within the receiving facility. Have

the central receiving warehouse area alarmed and monitored by the campus law enforcement department.

9. Ensure shrubs and others trees adjacent to the warehouse or compound area are kept trimmed.

10. Have a safe available on-site at the central receiving area. Maintain accurate inventories upon receipt and dispersal of goods.

Practices such as these will significantly reduce the opportunities for crimes to occur in the procurement department.

Finance Department

Some of the services which are provided by finance departments on campus include cashiering, accounting, payroll, property, accounts payable, and accounts receivable. In this grouping of service functions, there are obviously some areas which provide potential opportunity for serious crimes. Theft, burglary, and armed robbery are possible crimes related to finance departments on campuses today.

Many crime prevention measures can be employed by the finance department as a normal part of doing business. For example, it is important to periodically check the condition of doors and windows as well as their frames in the finance department facility. Windows and doors should be alarmed and the alarm should be monitored in the campus law enforcement department. Adequate lighting should be present outside of the finance department. Lights can be left on inside the finance department work area at night or after business hours. At the end of the workday, cash drawers should be left open and empty with all cash secured in an alarmed safe. The combination to the safe should be periodically changed. It must be automatically changed when someone who knows the combination is transferred to another department, resigns or is fired. Consideration should be given to installing closed-circuit television monitors in the finance department work area, lobby and safe location. Personnel working in the finance department should be carefully screened regarding questions of integrity before being hired, and after being employed should be given training in robbery and burglary prevention. All personnel entering the finance department should be required to enter and exit through single entry points. Additional exit points should be marked for emergency only and be alarmed. Any cash receipts kept in the finance department should be kept to a minimum and safely stored prior to being deposited at banks. Bank deposit times and routes should be varied. A holdup or panic alarm system should be installed in the finance department with adequate instructions for all staff on how and when to activate the system.

The Campus Bookstore

The campus bookstore which frequently operates in much the same way as a small retail department store has many points of vulnerability regarding criminal acts. The campus bookstore has a significant role to play in the prevention of crimes such as theft, burglary, armed robbery, shoplifting, and employee internal thefts.

Some of the crime prevention practices which have been found to be effective in the operation of campus bookstores are discussed as follows. Campus bookstore employees should receive training regarding the prevention of all the crimes mentioned in the preceding paragraph. They should in particular be taught to be alert for suspicious persons as well as what to do in the event of an armed robbery. Holdup or panic alarms should be located near the cash-handling areas of a bookstore. Only the minimum amount of cash necessary to operate the business should be maintained in the cash registers. Cash in excess of a designated minimum amount should be deposited frequently and stored in a secured alarmed safe on the premises prior to being deposited in local banking facilities. Cash-handling procedures should be varied in order to reduce predictable patterns from being established. Cash should never be left unattended. Cash drawers should be left open once emptied at night. Emergency telephone stickers should be placed on all telephones in the bookstore. The condition of all doors and windows should be checked to be certain that they meet security standards. Skylights and outside vents should be secured. Lights should be left on inside the campus bookstore at night, and all lights external to the entries and windows to the campus bookstore should be adequately maintained. Burglar alarms should be placed on the windows of the campus bookstore as well as any exterior doors. The alarms should be monitored by the campus law enforcement department. Consideration should be given to installing closed-circuit television monitors at all cash-handling points as well as in the safe room of the campus bookstore.

Campus bookstore employees should be educated regarding shoplifters and shoplifting techniques. Bookstore clerks should be alert to switched price tags on sale items. Trash containers which may contain stolen items to be later picked up should be checked periodically. One of the best approaches to deter potential shoplifters is for the bookstore clerks to acknowledge all customers' presence and to offer assistance. Managers of bookstores should consider rewarding employees who are active in crime prevention. Bookstore personnel should be educated regarding the link between retail loss, store profits, and overall salary structures. Bookstore supervisors should enforce rules and have clear-cut disciplinary guidelines regarding thefts or security breaches. Clerks and supervisors in bookstore operations should adopt a zero-shortage attitude.

Campus Intercollegiate Athletic And Recreational/intramural Department

On some campuses, the intercollegiate athletic and recreation departments are separate programs. For the purposes of this discussion, they will be treated as one department because many of the crime prevention issues would be similar. The campus intercollegiate athletic and recreation department is designed to provide a wide variety of sports and recreational activities for the entire campus community. While many of the events will not involve large numbers of people, some of them will and some of the events, by their very nature, will create security concerns. Unfortunately, at many athletic or other sporting events, it is not uncommon to hear of alcohol- or drug-related crimes, assaults, spectator violence, armed robberies, thefts, or burglaries occurring. The athletic department can take an active role in the prevention of many of these acts through adequate preplanning with the campus law enforcement agency.

There are many important factors to consider in the preplanning of athletic events. For example, it is very important that once an event has been scheduled that the campus law enforcement agency be consulted. Issues such as the purpose of the event, who is expected to be in attendance, and the anticipated crowd size are all critical in terms of security planning. The answers to those questions will help determine the number of security personnel which will be necessary for the event, whether there will be a need to have sworn officers with arrest authority or only non-sworn security personnel present.

Other important factors for security preplanning include the starting and ending time of the event, where the event is to actually be physically located, and accommodations for adequate parking. The security of those parked vehicles will also be a necessary issue to discuss in advance of the event itself. If cash is to be collected, the cash handlers will need to know what to do in the event they are approached by an armed robber and how to summon assistance from the campus law enforcement agency. A determination will need to be made as to how to handle unruly spectators (e.g., arrest, trespass or both). State statutes regarding alcohol possession/consumption and trespassing must be examined for relevance.

It is also helpful to review the frequency and nature of criminal incidents at similar athletic events or at the same athletic event in prior years. In all likelihood, if the event is going to be large one, additional assistance from local community law enforcement and emergency services units will be necessary. These issues as well as many others should be discussed and resolved well in advance of the athletic special event occurring.

Audiovisual Department

The audiovisual department on many campuses is extremely important as a support unit to the academic instructional areas. Video recorders, tape players, televisions, and 16mm projectors are all used extensively throughout colleges today. All too often the academic departments suffer as a result of audiovisual thefts. For example, it is not uncommon to hear of thefts, burglaries, and even internal pilferage of sophisticated audiovisual equipment. Many times, the responsibility for the equipment is mutually shared between the audiovisual department and the instructional personnel making use of the equipment.

Certain crime prevention practices will minimize the opportunity for theft. For example, if audiovisual equipment is to be left unattended after use in a classroom, the doors should be closed and locked when the instructor leaves. Should it be impossible to lock the door, equipment should be stored out of sight or, if practical, taken with the instructor to a location more secure than the classroom. Audiovisual supervisors should periodically visit classrooms to ensure proper measures of security are being employed with the audiovisual equipment. Supervisors should also talk to instructional personnel and academic department chairpersons to emphasize their role in the crime prevention efforts regarding audiovisual equipment.

All audiovisual equipment should be clearly labeled as property of the college and be marked in such a fashion so it can be easily identified and retrieved. The audiovisual department area should have a single entrance and exit to the area where the equipment is housed. This entrance should be monitored at all times and all other exits should be alarmed doors. There should be careful accounting and documentation of all audiovisual equipment when it leaves the department. Consideration should be given to alarming all windows and doors in the audiovisual storage area and having the alarms monitored by the campus law enforcement agency.

Key Control Department

There are a wide variety of departments that can have the responsibility for key control. Key control policy and issuance may be a responsibility of the campus law enforcement department, physical plant department, the campus business office, or some other department. Obviously, good key control provides a critical foundation for any efforts at campus crime prevention. Thefts, burglaries, and physical or sexual assaults may result if inadequate key control is inadequate or policies are not properly promulgated or followed. While a central campus department may be responsible for developing a key control policy and issuing keys, department administrators, individual staff and faculty should be held accountable for employing proper safeguards relative to keys under their supervision.

The decisions regarding which type of key control system should be used and who should actually receive certain keys are very important issues. There are, of course, locking systems which are either mechanical or electronic in nature. Electronic systems are generally regarded as being more sophisticated from a security standpoint. However, in many cases and on many campuses, mechanical key systems are the only ones affordable. Many campuses employ a master key system throughout their institution and use additional safeguards for specific buildings or units within buildings by means of electronic or mechanical locking systems.

Some general principals apply in virtually any key system which may be present in an institutional setting. For example, there should be strict controls over the issuance and retrieval of keys. Signature authorization should be required by an accountable officer before a new employee may obtain a key or before a current employee is provided with additional keys. The employee receiving the key should be sent to a central key-issuing location and required to show not only their administrative officers signature but also their own photo identification. Each key issued should be stamped with an individual identification number and should be assigned to a specific employee with a record maintained by the key-issuing office. Keys should never identify the building or specific room to which it belongs.

Institutional keys which are thought to be stolen or lost should be reported immediately to a supervisor and campus law enforcement agency. Consideration should be given to rekeying the area directly affected if the lost or stolen key may access what is considered a high-security area. Campus employees who fail to exercise due care in the custody of their keys should receive administrative sanctions from their supervisors. Prior to the issuance of their final paycheck, all employees resigning from the institution should be required to return their key to their supervisor. If an employee is dismissed from the institution, the key should be retrieved immediately by their supervisor.

General Key Control Issues

Exterior door keys for campus buildings should be issued on a limited basis. Generally speaking, the fewer personnel who have exterior door keys, the more secure the overall facility is. Individuals who are authorized to have keys to exterior building doors should not automatically be issued master keys to all interior units of the building. If access is needed to the locked building after normal work hours, the campus law enforcement agency should be provided with a list of authorized personnel who are permitted access after those hours. If entry by authorized personnel is allowed after normal business hours, a written log should be maintained on all persons entering and exiting these buildings. The campus law enforcement agency may prefer to send their representative to allow the authorized individual access building or may maintain centrally a key to be checked out by those persons.

Interior Key Control

Cabinets within offices which are used to maintain keys should be kept locked and located in a secure area at all times. Generally speaking, employees should be issued keys which will access only their work area unless entry to additional offices is needed on a regular basis. For example, it may not be necessary to give all staff members who work in a particular unit the key to everyone else's office space within that unit. This practice helps to maintain the integrity of individual office space.

Some offices are considered high-security areas. For example, this may be an area in which petty cash is maintained or expensive video equipment may be present. Likewise, the student health center pharmacy area may have drugs or other paraphernalia present which requires that additional security measures be taken. The high-security space may be an office, a storage room, or even a closet inside of offices or classrooms. An employee may be issued a key which allows access to a particular office but not necessarily be issued a key to a high-security closet or space within that office. The need to gain periodic access to equipment in a secure area does not necessarily justify an individual being issued a key to that area. These decisions must be carefully reviewed by departmental supervisors and not made solely on the basis of providing ready access to all persons making the request. Frequently, in campus settings many personnel are of the opinion that they need absolute access to most areas at all times. If such a practice is followed, there will, in all likelihood, be very little integrity in the building security system of the campus.

CAMPUS EMPLOYEE SECURITY ISSUES

The managers and supervisors of a campus should be aware that not all campus crimes are committed by outsiders or students. In some cases, campus employees have become involved in criminal acts. Some employees who have committed crimes within their respective institutions have attempted to rationalize their responsibility in having committed the crime itself. That is to say, they did not really "steal" the property but merely borrowed it for personal use for a given period of time. The article "did not belong to anyone." It was there for "everyone's use." It is also not unheard of for campus employees to disregard security rules and practices or even overlook thefts being committed by others.

It is important that the campus policymakers consider how to handle employee security issues. It is very useful to have a written policy regarding security which outlines all staff members' responsibilities and establishes disciplinary guidelines regarding non-adherence to those responsibilities. The administrators must also ensure that if such a policy exists it will be equitably applied throughout the various classifications of campus staff members. Campus employees should also be trained in proper security procedures. Many times, these employees will also be able to provide important input regarding security-related problems in a given work area. It is incumbent upon campus supervisors to solicit this input and to take steps to remedy problems as they are made known. The entire campus should work toward developing a "zero-shortage" attitude. The tone is set from the top of the campus organization—that management and supervisors care and that security of the institution is extremely important.

Managers and supervisors should also be aware of certain behaviors on the part of their subordinates which might be indicative of potential security-related problems. For example, many employees arrested for having committed crimes on campuses also have poor attendance records, are frequently late for work, and have been the subject of complaints by coworkers or members of the campus community served. Other signs which the supervisor should be aware of that may indicate a potential security problem with an employee are follows: An employee who is extremely vague in answering questions related to missing property or money; there are repeated inventory shortages in a given work unit; financial records which have obviously been rewritten or altered; an employee who has placed a personal check or IOU in the petty-cash box. While each of these situations may have a legitimate explanation, they may also be indicative of a more complex security breach. Supervisors and managers should immediately contact their campus law enforcement department to determine the best approach in these situations. Too frequently, the campus law enforcement agency is called in to assist, only to find valuable evidence has been destroyed or inappropriately dealt with.

EMPLOYEE SCREENING AND SELECTION

One of the critical roles played by all supervisors in the campus setting is that of hiring honest, skilled staff members. Most hiring authorities agree that the single best predictor of future job success is performance on prior jobs. Therefore, it is worth the time and effort for supervisors and managers to check out the prior work and academic records of potential employees. It is always useful, for example, to verify academic records and to speak to former employers. Some states and municipalities will allow fingerprint checks to be conducted for certain positions. The circumstances surrounding any recorded felony conviction should be closely reviewed if an applicant is still under consideration. The campus should have a policy which speaks to these issues.

In talking with a former employer regarding a job applicant, supervisors may legitimately inquire into a number of specific areas. For example, it might be useful to ask the former employer if there were standards for integrity and honesty in the employee's prior position. The hiring authority may also wish to find out information relative to the following: What was the applicant's attitude towards security? Was there a record of prior discipline? If prior disciplinary actions had been taken against the employee, what were the circumstances? Was there ever any reason to doubt the applicant's honesty or integrity on the job? Each of these areas are important subjects to discuss with prior employers before making a job offer. Campus managers and supervisors should review these issues with their legal advisor's office prior to finalizing their applicant-selection process. However, one question which generally may assist the supervisor in reaching a hiring decision is, "Would you hire this person again?" A negative response, a hesitancy to respond, or a failure to respond to this question on the part of a prior employer should be deemed very significant by the campus manager.

SUGGESTED SECURITY QUESTIONS

1. Does the campus law enforcement department have a proactive crime prevention program?
2. Does the campus law enforcement department establish crime prevention objectives?
3. Do the crime prevention programs attempt to generate campus community involvement?
4. Does upper-level campus administration actively support ongoing crime prevention efforts and programs?
5. Does the campus have crime prevention programs similar to Neighborhood Watch actively operating in their residence halls and academic buildings?
6. Does the campus law enforcement department use new student and employee orientation programs to encourage crime prevention practices?
7. Is an active crime prevention program ongoing in the student residence halls?
8. Does the campus law enforcement department provide personal safety/rape prevention programs for faculty, students, and staff on campus?
9. Does the campus law enforcement department actively seek information regarding crimes that have occurred adjacent to the campus from other law enforcement agencies?
10. Has the campus been surveyed regarding areas potentially vulnerable to criminal acts?
11. Does the campus routinely conduct lighting surveys and follow-up and correct deficiencies identified?

12. Does the campus have emergency telephones or other emergency-signalling devices available throughout the campus?
13. Is it policy to secure campus office buildings when they are not occupied?
14. What are the existing key control and issuance policies of the campus?
15. Has the campus administration actively encouraged departments such as student life, campus law enforcement, physical plant, legal affairs, resident life, and others to be cooperatively involved in crime prevention efforts?

ENDNOTES

1. Sewell, James D. Crime on campus: Legal and administrative issues involving homicide and assault. In Leonard Territo and Max L. Bromley (Eds.), *Hospital and College Security Liability*, Columbia, MD: Hanrow Press, 1987, pp. 191–192.
2. Territo, Leonard. Selecting the security expert." In Leonard Territo and Max L. Bromley (Eds.), *Hospital and College Security Liability*, Columbia, MD: Hanrow Press, 1987, p. 259.
3. Nichols, David. *The Administration of Public Safety in Higher Education.* Springfield, Il: Charles C Thomas, 1987, p. 206.

SELECT CASES

Siciliano V. State, No. 712-895 (Super.Ct.CA1.)
Mullins V. Pine Manor College, 389 Mass. 47, 449 N.E. 2d 331, 11 Educ. L. Rep. 595 (1983).

Chapter 3

CRITICAL ISSUES IN
CAMPUS SECURITY AND SAFETY

In this chapter, we will discuss with the reader a series of important issues related to safety and security on college campuses. All of these issues are faced in varying degrees at both two- and four-year colleges and are generally applicable in both private and public institutions. Campus administrators, students, and faculty may well be directly involved in these issues and have an impact on how they are addressed on a campus.

We will provide the reader with information on how to involve students and campus staff in crime prevention programs such as the use of security teams, security and safety issues in campus residence halls (dormitories), campus alcohol/drug issues, and the steps campus administrators can take to ensure a proactive approach to campus security and crime prevention.

INVOLVING STUDENTS IN CRIME PREVENTION PROGRAMS

Campus administrators and campus law enforcement officials frequently search for ways to actively involve students in the overall crime prevention effort. Once a decision has been made to involve students in the programming efforts, topics must be identified which will have both general applicability and relevant information. Reviewing the last six to twelve month's reports regarding the nature, type and frequency of criminal activity on the campus generally provides a framework of reference upon which to build crime prevention efforts. If students are to be the primary audience of these programs, it would be advantageous to involve the students in the development of those programs. Topics for inclusion in the program can be quite varied depending upon the past criminal incidents on campus and the desires of the students involved.

Crime prevention programs typically cover the following topics: dorm theft prevention; bike theft prevention; personal safety awareness; creating positive community/campus law enforcement relations; and drug/

alcohol education programs. Each of these topics are somewhat distinctive in nature and are examples of the kinds of criminal acts which frequently occur on campus. Campus law enforcement agencies and student life representatives frequently work together in developing the details of the programs. Students are often used in the development of the program as it relates to both content and delivery. Many campuses use students as the "actors" if slides are to be prepared as part of the programs. A multipurpose slide show or video program can be developed which will provide information regarding the various crime prevention topics listed earlier.

Neighborhoods throughout the country have developed citizen "crime watch" programs. Similar crime watch programs are now in practice on many campuses in student residence halls. The emphasis of these programs is for individuals to assume a degree of personal responsibility and develop an interest in the safety, security and the welfare of fellow residents. Commonsense precautions are generally part of the information distributed relative to the prevention of crimes which typically occur in the student residence halls. Many campus law enforcement agencies, at the beginning of each college term, will go door to door in the campus residence halls and offer engraving services for students' personal items. Students' bicycles are frequently registered on-site in the dormitory. Generally, engraving of personal items and their registration have been found to be effective in crime prevention efforts and in the recovery of those items should they be stolen.

Campuses can be very creative in their efforts to involve students in crime prevention program. Some colleges actually sponsor a "crime prevention contest" which encourages members of the student population to suggest new crime prevention tips and techniques. The on-campus food service or local merchants, such as bike shops, may be contacted to offer prizes for the best ideas provided. T-shirts which display crime prevention slogans are popular on some campuses.

Funding sources for many student crime prevention programs may be found throughout the campus community. For example, involving student government, student social/fraternity organizations, or groups such as ROTC are excellent ways to develop broad-based support and identify additional financial resources. Students may also be used to help develop crime prevention efforts as part of their class assignment projects. For example, art students may be active in the development of brochures or posters. Public relations or communications students may help to develop literature for the crime prevention programs. These assignments can often be made as part of a class project if detailed well in advance of the class beginning.

Crime prevention messages can be widely distributed in a rather inexpensive manner. For example, these tips can appear on book markers, pencils, placemats which appear in student cafeterias, or on napkins. These items are relatively inexpensive to buy in bulk, with the crime prevention information mass produced on their face. Crime prevention messages may also be delivered in other ways. For example, one campus placed parking tickets on the windshields of all vehicles parked in their student lots on the week before a major holiday. As anyone knows who has received one, a parking ticket on one's windshield gets your attention quickly.[1] However, the parking tickets had driver safety tips rather than the standard parking violation information. This method was indeed an attention getter. Some campuses now use the "hang tag" method of vehicle registration as opposed to placing an adhesive decal on the bumper of the vehicle. These hang tags which are usually hooked to the rearview mirror inside the vehicle may have a simple crime prevention tip such as "Lock your car." Crime prevention tips may also be stamped on the signs which appear in parking lots, for example, "Lock your car as you leave it."

Some campuses have become quite creative in their approach to providing crime prevention information. For example, one college placed monthly crime prevention posters on the inside doors of the stalls in restrooms throughout the campus. The crime prevention posters became known quickly as "stall stories." Another campus developed a crime prevention mascot who regularly appeared in a comic strip in the campus newspaper. Other campuses routinely write a "police beat" column in their campus newspapers or take out a crime prevention ad. There are, obviously, many ways to send crime prevention messages to the student population.

Many campuses throughout the country have established student security programs. These programs supplement the campus law enforcement agency and serve a very active role. Functions frequently served by the student security officers include: escorts, communications support, special events security, and other miscellaneous services. The student security programs which have traditionally met with the most success have been comprised of students who were paid, carefully selected, given adequate training, and usually supplied with some form of distinctive uniform. Student security officers may also provide useful services such as distributing crime prevention brochures and posters and placing emergency telephone decals on telephones throughout the campus.

The campus law enforcement agency plays a key role in the involvement of students in crime prevention efforts. One technique found to be useful on many campuses is the initiation of a student "ride along" program. In this program the campus law enforcement agency actually encourages students to spend part of a duty shift with one of their officers in order to view firsthand the role of campus law enforcement. When such a program is first initiated, many campus law enforcement departments have taken the time to invite key student leaders such as the student newspaper editor to participate in the program or the student government president. Many campuses have active women's groups. These women's groups can provide a great deal of assistance to the campus law enforcement department in the development of many crime prevention programs, particularly those that relate to personal safety issues. Campus law enforcement representatives should seek out every opportunity to speak to residence hall students, commuter students, new student orientation programs, and even academic classes when appropriate regarding crime prevention and public safety issues. Many campus law enforcement agencies are required to conduct annual auctions of found property. Students should be involved in the auction process, and the proceeds from the auction may be used to support student-related crime prevention efforts and programs.

One group that is closely related to students on campus but often overlooked in the crime prevention effort is parents. If the college holds parent open houses or parent orientation programs, this is a good opportunity for the campus law enforcement agency to make crime prevention presentations. This can also provide a forum to answer questions and concerns which parent of current or future students may have. This provides an excellent opportunity to show true concern for safety and security issues to the parents of students. The parents can also be provided with realistic information regarding the fact that campuses are not exempt from criminal incidents, and commonsense prevention methods should be practiced.

INVOLVING CAMPUS STAFF IN CRIME PREVENTION PROGRAMS

In addition to involving students in campus safety and security issues and the prevention of criminal acts, it is advantageous to involve the staff of the college in similar programs. For example, some campuses have provided crime prevention training sessions for members of the grounds maintenance department, housekeepers, custodial personnel, physical plant and maintenance employees, and parking ticket writers. Each of these personnel are widely dispersed through the campus grounds, parking lots, and buildings. They are in an ideal situation to serve as "eyes and ears" for the campus crime prevention program. If campus maintenance vehicles are equipped with citizen band radios connected to the campus law enforcement department, it is easy for maintenance personnel to communicate suspicious activities and persons in an efficient manner. These groups of employees should be provided with information related to what is considered a suspicious activity or person, and how to report the same. In addition, they are in good positions to identify potential safety or security hazards which need correction.

It is important that if campus staff members such as those described above are to become involved in the campus crime prevention effort, adequate reinforcement of their positive actions will be necessary. This reinforcement can be accomplished in a variety of ways. Written commendations, financial reward, awarding donated prizes, providing a free meal at the on-campus food serviced, and highlighting their overall crime prevention efforts in the campus newspaper are effective means of reinforcement.

Some colleges have initiated a program of "foot patrol" on the part of their campus law enforcement officers. Frequently, officers will be encouraged to leave their vehicles to walk the campus grounds and to make their presence known inside of buildings. Officers may actually be assigned specific facilities for periodic checks and contacts. Officers may be encouraged to get to know campus staff members working within the buildings and to provide crime prevention information as appropriate. For example, campus law enforcement officers assigned to a particular building may distribute brochures regarding office theft prevention tips or place emergency phone stickers on each extension within the office. Wallet-sized cards may be provided to staff members working within office areas which include information regarding crime prevention tips and emergency phone numbers.

After normal working hours, officers may check assigned areas for security deficiencies. If, for example, an office door is found unlocked, an officer may leave a card at that site indicating the lack of security was found and asking for a return of the card by the person occupying the office to indicate that the information was received. Similar to the student residence hall crime watch programs, a "building crime watch" program may be initiated. Office staff members are provided with crime prevention and other security-related information and are asked to assist in the reduction of office crimes. The campus law enforcement agency may work with secretarial staff and supervisors on issues such as key control, petty cash security, and office equipment security techniques.

Campus staff members are usually very willing to become involved in crime prevention programs which have application both in the institutional setting and at home. For example, many campuses now offer personal safety and home security programs for their staff members. Some campus law enforcement departments have sponsored child safety programs wherein staff members may bring their children to work on a Saturday for a crime prevention presentation and fingerprinting. Campus staff members may be willing to become directly involved in the campus law enforcement effort by serving as reserve officers. In this capacity, the campus staff member will perform many of the same functions listed for the student security officer earlier in this chapter. Staff members may also be involved in a citizens band radio crime prevention program. In these programs, they are encouraged to contact the campus law enforcement department if they observe a criminal act or other suspicious activity while in their vehicle on campus.

As mentioned in Chapter 2, staff members who work in retail-type facilities such as the campus bookstore or in cash-handling areas, such as the finance department, should receive additional crime prevention training in the areas of theft prevention, armed robbery prevention, and shoplifting prevention. One campus law enforcement department with the cooperation of the campus bookstore manager demonstrated how easy it was for individuals to shoplift merchandise from the store. Campus law enforcement officers dressed in civilian attire were sent into the bookstore for a period of less than an hour. Their instructions were to shoplift all items which they could readily get their hands on in the period of time they were in the bookstore. At the end of the designated time, all items stolen were taken to the bookstore manager's office and placed on a table. After the shoplifted merchandise was placed on the table, the bookstore clerks were invited in to see what had happened. Needless to say, a distinct impression was made at that time and everyone agreed additional shoplifting prevention training was necessary.

Campus law enforcement agencies have developed a number of methods for distributing crime prevention information in addition to those mentioned earlier. One example is the development of a staff crime prevention newsletter. This newsletter is circulated to all employees within the college community and posted in numerous locations. The newsletter contains information regarding crimes which have or may occur on campus, reminders of commonsense crime prevention tips, and include the answers to questions frequently to the campus law enforcement department by members of the community. Some campus law enforcement agencies provide information to recently hired staff members at new employee orientation programs. Other crime prevention literature may be distributed at the new employee payroll or benefits sign-up office. Crime prevention tips and information may be enclosed with the envelope in which staff members receive their paycheck. Campuses which have an employee union may find it useful to ask the organization for space in their literature which is periodically distributed to its membership. The obvious need to involve campus staff in safety, security and crime prevention measures is obvious and the effort to-do so can result in significant dividends for the overall community.

STUDENT RESIDENCE HALL SECURITY AND SAFETY ISSUES

On some campuses, students who live in residence halls comprise a significant proportion of the total enrollment. Even on campuses which are not heavily populated with on-campus residents, student housing represents a significant security and safety concern. Prior to a further discussion of these issues, two points should be made for the reader. Today's on-campus residence halls appear in a variety of shapes and sizes. For example, there are the traditional high-rise dormitories which were prevalent in the fifties and sixties on college campuses. At the other extreme, there are apartment-like residence living arrangements which increased with popularity in the sixties and seventies. The reader should also keep in mind that while some student residence halls are contemporary in design and reflect modern-day security technology, many campus dorms were built well over 60 years ago and are much more difficult to secure. Therefore, it is very difficult to describe the typical student resident living facility. This variation necessitates that further discussion of security and safety issues in student resident facilities to be somewhat general in nature. It is, however, safe to assume that the safety and security of students living on campus is an extremely high priority with campus student-life officials and law enforcement personnel.

It is well established that many crimes committed on today's college campuses occur within the student resident living facilities. For example, assaults, burglary, rape, and thefts are not uncommon in the student residence halls. If one examines many of the dormitories we see on our campuses, there are ample opportunities for these crimes to occur. The physical layout of a facility frequently adds or detracts from potential security problems. For example, in a high-rise dormitory of eight or nine stories, it is extremely important for students living on one floor to know the residents on another. There is, by virtue of the design of the facility, a degree of anonymity which often provides ample opportunity for crimes to occur.

There is also the problem on many of our campuses of transients who are not affiliated with the college but who are sharing living accommodations within student residence halls. Students are frequently manipulated into allowing non-affiliates to live in the residence halls for a short period of time. Frequently, these transients commit numerous criminal acts prior to moving on to other living accommodations. It is often several days before the student residents recognize that they have been victimized by the individuals who they naively allowed to live in their room. Other times, crimes of a more serious nature have occurred as a result of allowing non-affiliates to live in the campus residence halls.

The courts have also become quite concerned about issues relating to student residence hall security. Liability suits have been brought before courts alleging that an institution failed to provide an adequate level of security for the students living in the residence halls. For example, in *Duarte v. State* (1979), the courts decided that a university could be found liable for the rape and murder of a student in a dormitory because a special landlord-tenant relationship between the institution and student existed. Furthermore, the university was negligent, in that it had misrepresented the safety of the campus.[1] A second case, *Miller v. State*, in 1985, established that the university's failure to lock outer doors of a dormitory was a breach of duty and the proximate cause of a rape of a student. Furthermore, this same court increased the original award to the plaintiff of $25,000 to $400,000 because of the horror and consequences of the rape.[2] Given the nature and frequency of crimes being committed in our student resident living facilities and the subsequent liability which may be attached to the institution, it is readily apparent that those officials associated with campus student living must establish proactive programs to enhance the security and safety of student residence halls.

One researcher suggests that campus administrators should have a planned approach to addressing residence halls security issues.

> The first step should be to update or create a document that clearly represents the institution's position on residence hall security. The position document should enumerate the standards for each residence hall, for instance whether the exterior doors will be locked, whether alarm systems are to be utilized, will be security desks be in place, and whether emergency phones are to be available. . . . The second step that must be initiated is a self-assessment of the security operation and programs for the campus residence halls.[3]

Physical Security In Residence Halls

After the decision has been made by campus administrators to establish a security plan for residence halls, it is important that the physical security (e.g., locks, lights) of those residence halls be examined. This self-examination will help those officials in charge of the residence halls to make a series of security-related decisions. For instance, before selecting a new locking system for a student housing complex at the University of Alaska in Anchorage, campus officials considered the security needs of the students living there. The system installed there used a device which resembled a key but contained a magnetic strip that was specifically coded. Each lock in the University of Alaska system was programed to accept only keys with a specific code. The on-campus key shop was able to meet the needs of their system. This program helped reduce the duplication of residence hall keys. The system also raised the security awareness of the students living in the dormitories and underscored the role that they play in keeping the residence halls secure.[4]

Additional physical security issues should be reviewed in the student residence hall facilities. For example, are the individual dorm rooms equipped with specialized security devices such as peepholes in the door, or combination-type locking devices? It is important that the shrubs and trees adjacent to the student residence halls be kept closely trimmed to eliminate places of concealment for would-be assailants. Dormitory lights, both internal and external, should be checked periodically. This is very critical in areas adjacent to entryways and exits to the residence halls. Lights found to be inoperative should be repaired properly and all actions adequately documented. Student residence hall laundry rooms and vending machine areas are frequently found in isolated parts of the facility. Are these rooms monitored from a security standpoint and how are they eventually secured? It is very important that the exterior doors to the student dormitory be in good repair and have adequate locking mechanisms. Exterior doors which are required to be locked from the outside after certain hours should be equipped with alarms which will annunciate if opened from the inside or outside. Some student residence halls are equipped with closed-circuit television cameras which monitor critical security areas during certain hours of operation.

Procedural Security Issues

In addition to reviewing the physical security of the student residence halls, it is important for the campus administrators to examine procedural issues related to security in the student residence halls. For example, once security devices (e.g., locks, alarms) have been installed, it is essential that students be formally made aware of the devices, the importance for using them correctly, and the expectations made clear that it is the students' responsibility to use them properly. One of the questions which is frequently asked is "Who is actually responsible for providing security in campus residence halls?" In fact, the responsibility is shared by the student residents, officials in charge of the residence halls, the campus law enforcement department, and ultimately the top-level administration.

However, individual responsibilities should be made as clear as possible. For example, it is good procedure to lock the exterior doors to campus residence halls during evening hours. As a follow-up to that procedure, the person responsible for making periodic checks of exterior doors after they are secure should be clearly identified. The frequency of the security checks for these exterior doors must be established. Another recommended procedure is to require that dorm residents and their visitors be required to enter the residence hall through a controlled centralized entry point after the hours of nightfall. The decision must then be made as to how best to monitor this practice and ensure its compliance. Many colleges employ residence hall lobby monitors for this purpose. If the student residence hall has rules restricting the access of non-residents, these rules should be made clear to all and enforced. The residence hall programs should have a process established to deal quickly and fairly with students who have violated security procedures and jeopardized the welfare of their fellow residents.

The residence hall should have a procedure to deal with students who have committed property-related infractions or minor crimes in the dorms. For example, some universities have developed a "damage reduction model" to combat the increasing costs of vandalism in the student residence halls. In these programs, residence hall staff members meet with the residents to discuss vandalism and attempt to redirect this type of negative and destructive behavior. This is an effort intended to get students to feel better about their living environment and to provide them a forum regarding their problems in the residence halls. Any damage committed in the residence halls is quickly repaired. This type of program attempts to reduce vandalism by having procedures in place to improve communication and to repair damaged properties as soon as possible.[5]

At a very minimum, procedures should be in place that ensure close cooperation and interaction between the campus law enforcement department and those officials responsible for managing the student residence halls. Representatives from the campus law enforcement department should routinely conduct crime prevention/education programs for resident students. Resident students should be adequately informed about security and safety procedures which apply in the residence halls. All students should receive training in how to react and how to seek aid when serious incidents occur in their residence halls. Procedures should be very clear regarding when the campus law enforcement department is to be summoned for assistance. The responsibilities of the campus law enforcement representative upon arrival at the student residence hall, and those of the student residence life officials, should be clearly understood in advance.

The following security procedures are examples of those frequently given to students living in campus residence halls:

1. Do not prop open locked exterior residence hall doors.
2. Lock the residence hall room door when sleeping.
3. Lock the residence hall room door when leaving a roommate asleep inside.
4. Lock the residence room hall door when leaving regardless of the length of time anticipated being gone.

5. Keep small items of value such as wallets, purses, money, and jewelry out of sight.
6. Engrave all valuable items with a number which distinctly identifies you, and keep a record of all valuables noting their description and serial numbers. Frequently, this distinctive identification number is the individual's driver's license number. Engravers can usually be borrowed from the campus law enforcement agency.
7. Mark all clothing with a laundry pencil or needle and thread in a place other than the label.
8. Do not leave notes on the residence hall door announcing that no one is home.
9. Do not place decals on the residence hall door announcing the names of the persons who live there.
10. Do not take in overnight guests who are unknown.
11. Do not allow door-to-door salespersons to enter the residence hall room. This alleged salesperson may be "casing the room" for a later theft or burglary.
12. Require identification and authorization from maintenance staff members who allege to be in the residence hall room on official business.
13. Do not loan the residence hall room key or have duplicates made.
14. Report all thefts or other crimes committed immediately to the campus law enforcement agency.
15. Report to the residence hall staff all doors, locks, windows, or lights that are in need of repair.
16. Be suspicious of unknown persons loitering or checking doors in the residence halls. Note their description and call the campus law enforcement department immediately.[6]

Many campus residence hall rooms are equipped with private telephones for the students. It is not uncommon for students living in residence halls to be victimized by nuisance or obscene telephone callers. Some of the recommended procedures for dealing with this type of telephone call are listed as follows:

1. Hang up the telephone as soon as an obscenity or improper question or suggestion is made.
2. Do not play detective. Do not extend the call trying to figure out who is doing the calling. This is the type of reaction the caller wants and needs.

3. Do not try to be clever. The response may be interpreted as encouragement.
4. Do not play counselor. The caller may need professional help.
5. Do not let the caller know that you are angry or upset.
6. Everyone does not need to be told about the calls. Frequently, this type of call is actually made by friends or other acquaintaines.
7. Be careful when the caller says he or she is taking a survey. If there is any concern about the legitimacy of the call, obtain the caller's name, firm name, and business telephone number. Indicate that the objective of obtaining this information is to verify the authenticity of the survey.
8. Do not volunteer your name to an unknown caller.
9. Place ads in the newspaper with caution. Consider using a post office box for replies. If you must use your phone number, do not use your address.
10. Report obscene or annoying calls to the campus law enforcement department. Make a record of the calls by keeping a log if they continue. This log should record information such as the time of the call, the date of the call, the nature of the call (threat, obscene, nusiance), the sex and approximate age of the caller, and any other distinguishing characteristics regarding the caller's voice (nervous, accent, apparently intoxicated).[7]

Student Residence Hall Fire Safety Issues

On a nationwide basis, statistics reveal that the majority of fire deaths occur in residential structures. The campus residence hall is the student's home away from home during the period they are attending college. Therefore, there is obvious cause for concern regarding the potential for a serious fire in a campus residence hall situation. It is critical that issues relating to residence hall fire safety be addressed in adequate fashion by campus officials. Similar to the security issues which must be reviewed in on-campus residential structures, a strong fire safety program is also necessary. The following are suggested as minimal components for an effective residence hall fire safety program:

1. Develop a complete listing of all areas within the student residence hall facilities which contain potentially hazardous materials or explosives. Provide this information in advance to the campus law enforcement department and local fire department.

2. Provide the campus law enforcement department and local fire department with a set of completed drawings of the floor plans of the campus residence halls. Indicate in those drawings where fire-fighting equipment may be obtained.
3. Develop a comprehensive fire safety program for the student residence hall facilities. This should include a thorough review of all potential fire safety hazards including living units, lobbies, and maintenance areas.
4. Be aware of and in compliance with local, state, and federal fire safety requirements and standards.
5. Ensure that there is an open line of communication among the campus residence life staff, local fire department, and the campus law enforcement department. Have procedures developed in advance which indicate the individual responsibilities of those departments in the event of a fire in a residence hall facility.
6. Identify a residence hall staff member to be designated as a fire safety liaison. This person will coordinate closely with the on-campus safety officer, campus law enforcement department, and local fire officials within the community.
7. Ensure that there is adequate cooperation and sufficient support from residence hall administrative staff, students living in the facilities, and employees of the residence life department, in all fire safety and prevention issues.
8. Require frequent fire safety inspections within the student resident halls. Identify deficiencies to be overcome and ensure that follow-up is completed.
9. Ensure that full-time residence hall staff members and student resident assistants receive adequate training in fire prevention and the proper utilization of basic fire-fighting equipment such as extinguishers.
10. Provide information to residence hall students regarding fire safety on a periodic basis.
11. Ensure that fire drills are routinely conducted for all residence students. Fire safety drills are of great importance during the first few weeks of occupancy of their residence hall. New tenants at that point are not thoroughly familiar with points of egress within the residence hall.

Common Fire Hazards In Residence Hall Rooms

The following list was developed by the Northwestern University Department of Safety regarding fire hazards routinely discovered in campus residence hall facilities:

1. Decorations—combustible materials should not be permitted on the ceilings of residence hall rooms. Fishnets, Indian blankets or other such drapings should not be permitted on walls.
2. Electrical abuse—an electrical "octupus" can result in overloaded circuits and cause a fire. A damaged or overloaded extension can also cause a fire.
3. Appliances—popcorn poppers, coffee makers, and other cooking appliances should be prohibited in student resident rooms. Appliances should be unplugged when not in use.
4. Open flames—candles and other open-flame devices should not be permitted in student residence rooms, since they can easily ignite furnishings.
5. Smoking—smoking in bed should be prohibited in the student residence halls. In areas in the residence halls where smoking is permitted, good ashtrays should be made available. The ashtrays should never be emptied into wastebaskets until all contents are cool to the touch.
6. Flammable liquids—gasoline, paint thinner, and other flammable liquids should not be stored in any residential room. Vapors from these liquids may easily ignite and be explosive.
7. Hazardous storage—rubbish should be disposed of as soon as possible. Combustible materials should be stored in safe places away from potential heat sources.
8. Obstacles—bicycles, furniture, and other similar items should not be left in stairways or hallways or points of egress. All exit points within the residence halls should be kept clear at all times.[8]

Residence Hall Fire Safety Inspection

As mentioned earlier, the residence hall staff should conduct periodic fire safety inspections of all facilities. These inspections are conducted to ensure that all equipment is being adequately maintained and ready for use in the event of a fire. One university provides the following procedures for their residence hall fire safety inspections:

1. Exit lights shall be lighted at all times and shall have all lenses in place. Adequate stairway and corridor lights shall be lighted to provide enough light for safe travel. Lights must not be covered or otherwise obstructed in any way which will significantly reduce the light at floor level.
2. Panic bars on all exit doors shall operate normally.
3. Stairway doors shall automatically close and latch. They must be kept closed and never held open with wedges or other items.
4. Fire extinguishers shall be in proper locations, easily accessible, and in operating condition at all times.
5. Extinguisher and standpipe hose cabinet shall be closed, yet open easily. Glass, latches, and handles must be in good condition.
6. Fire alarm boxes shall be accessible and in good condition, and the system shall be operable at all times.
7. Exitways—interior and exterior—shall be unobstructive at all times.
8. Report any missing or defective equipment discovered to your housing office or the public safety office at once.[9]

What To Do In Case Of A Residence Hall Fire

Many colleges now provide resident students with a set of instructions regarding what to do if they discover a fire in their facility. While these instructions may vary from campus to campus relative to the specific types of facilities, much of the information is general in nature. The following instructions are provided at the University of Georgia:

1. Pull the nearest fire alarm and then call the emergency fire and campus law enforcement number. Remain calm, give your name and location of the fire (building and room number and what is burning, if known).
2. Evacuate the building using the corridors and stairwells. Close as many doors as possible between you and the fire.
3. Never use an elevator: power can fail and leave you stranded between floors in a burning building. Elevator shafts and open stairwells provide a chimney effect, drawing heat and smoke up the shaft.
4. If you encounter excessive smoke while evacuating the building, get as low as possible, and crawl to the nearest exit. Heat and smoke rise, so the coolest and cleanest air will be near the floor. If possible, cover your mouth and nose with a wet cloth, etc. to cool and partially filter the air you breathe.

5. If your primary exit becomes blocked, use a secondary exit. Once outside the building, move to a safe location from the building. Do not re-enter the building for anything until a fire official says it is alright to do so.

6. If you are in a building when the fire alarm sounds, remain calm. Proceed to the nearest exit using the procedures outlined above. If the door is closed in the room where you are located, do not open the door until you feel the knob and upper door for heat. If the knob and door are cool to the touch, brace yourself against the door and open slightly. Check conditions in the hall. If the hall does not contain excessive heat and smoke, proceed to the nearest exit using the procedures stated above. If there is excessive heat and smoke, remain in the room and follow the steps below:

a. If the knob and door is hot or even warm to the touch, do not open the door—there is a good chance the fire is in the hallway near your room and your probability of reaching the exit is very slim. Remain in your room. Stuff the cracks around the door with towels, etc. to keep out as much heat as possible.

b. Go to the window and, if it is clear outside (no smoke or flames), open the window at the top (to let out any heat or smoke in the room) and at the bottom (for a source of fresh air). Signal for help by hanging a flag (sheet, jacket, etc.) out the window. If there is a telephone in the room, call the fire department and police and advise them of your exact location, even if they are already on the scene. Never attempt to jump from a multistory building. Jumps from heights of three floors (36 feet or higher) are almost *always* fatal.[10]

Maintaining Life Safety In The Residence Halls

The University of Georgia Department of Public Safety also recommends the following regarding fire safety practices in their student residence halls which can be reviewed for adoption at other campuses.

1. *Stairwells—always keep stairwell doors closed. Do not* prop stairwell doors open. Smoke and heat rise and an open stairwell acts as a chimney rendering the stairwell unusable. *Never* store *anything* in or under a stairwell.

2. *Hallways—always keep hallways clear* of all obstructions. Keep smoke

and/or fire doors in hallways closed to retard the spread of heat, smoke, and flames in the event of fire.

3. Fire safety equipment—*do not* misuse or abuse fire extinguishers, pull stations, smoke and/or heat detectors, emergency lights, or sprinkler systems. Fire safety equipment is to be used in the time of a fire emergency (or *authorized* drills and tests).

4. Elevators—never use an elevator to evacuate the building in case of fire. A power failure can leave the elevator stranded between floors or open onto the fire floor. In addition, elevator shafts also act as a chimney in fire situations.[11]

Selection And Training Of Residence Hall Staff Members

An important aspect of the safety and security of student residence halls relates to the selection and training of staff members. While many student residence halls will have full-time professional persons who are responsible for the overall management of the dormitory, a student resident assistant will often be responsible for the day-to-day operations within the living units. The resident assistants have a difficult set of functions to perform in providing the peer leadership necessary. In many cases, the resident assistants are relied upon to make critical judgments that relate to the overall safety and security of the student residence hall. In most cases, the resident assistants must play dual roles—one of which is that of a counselor and the other is that of a police officer and disciplinarian. For example, while the resident assistant must provide support and understanding for the students living in the dormitory, they must also be prepared to enforce rules and regulations within the facility, many of which are unpopular with the resident students. The resident assistant is expected to help the students get adjusted to their new "home away from home" and to coordinate social activities for their facility. However, at the same time, the resident assistant is required to ensure that students will abide by policies of the residence halls which may include topics as wide ranging as alcohol and drug use, use of cooking appliances, tampering with fire and safety equipment, opening and closing room windows, restrictions on pets, opposite-sex visitation, and "quiet hours."

The diversity identified in the role expectations for the resident assistant are readily apparent. The selection of resident assistants is therefore made more critical. Some residence hall directors have involved not only other members of their residence hall staff but also members of other on-campus departments to help in the selection process. For example, a residence hall administrator may choose to involve staff of the campus counseling center or campus law enforcement department in the selection process for resident assistants. These two departments will work very closely with not only the residents but the residence hall staff on many issues of significance.

The majority of the persons that are chosen to be resident assistants are undergraduates. Most residence hall programs require that applicants for resident assistant positions be in good academic standing. The time and effort that the new resident assistants will spend in their jobs will necessitate that they have already developed good study habits and achieved a positive academic record. It is just as important that the new resident assistants be selected on the basis of having demonstrated good judgment in both personal situations and on prior jobs. The characteristics of maturity and leadership skills are generally thought to be very important in the selection of resident assistants. It is useful during the resident assistant interview process to present the applicants with hypothetical problems similar to the ones they will encounter in their new role. This approach requires the applicants to consider the issues they will be confronting as resident assistants and also provide the interviewers with an opportunity to see how the applicants will respond under pressure.

Once the new resident assistants have been selected, they should be involved in a training program which will help enhance the skills that will be necessary for them to be successful in their new role. There are a number of topics or issues which, from a safety and security standpoint, are very important for the new and the returning resident assistants to be familiar with. They should first and foremost be made aware of what their specific role is regarding the security and safety of the residence hall facility and students. It should be made very clear during this training what the expectations are regarding their proper role and what the limits are of those expectations. For example, the resident assistants need to know where all the security and safety equipment for the residence hall is located and how to properly use and maintain it. This would be true regarding items such as locks, alarms, fire extinguishers, and other related hardware. The new resident assistants should also be made to realize that they have a responsibility to notify their superior when any of this equipment is found to be inoperative.

Many campus residence hall directors will involve members of the campus law enforcement department in providing training regarding security issues. All resident assistants need to be informed as to the proper method of calling for assistance from the campus law enforcement department. They should be instructed when to call that department regarding medical, security, fire, or other critical incidents. Many times, it is useful during the training period to review cases which have occurred over the last several academic years to provide concrete examples of how the procedures should be followed. The resident assistant should be instructed that if there is a delay or hesitation in contacting the campus law enforcement department regarding a criminal act, this will only serve to reduce the overall security of the residence hall. Swift reporting of criminal incidents generally increases the chances of apprehension of offenders and the recovery of stolen property and may actually prevent another member of the residence hall population from being victimized.

The University of Delaware, Department of Public Safety, conducts just such training for the residence-life staff members. Specifically, they instruct residence hall staff members "that upon the discovery or observation of any actual or suspected criminal activity, whether in progress at the time or not, do not attempt to find out what is going on if you suspect criminal activity is taking place — call and allow us to respond and find out what is going on."[12] Further instructions regarding what to tell the radio dispatcher are as follows:

1. Name and telephone number.
2. Location of crime or suspected criminal activity.
3. Type of crime or activity.
4. Whether there are any injuries.
5. Whether the criminal or suspicious person is still there.
6. Where the victim of the crime can be located, if known.
7. A description of the criminal or suspicious person, if known.
8. What was stolen, if applicable.
9. Which way the criminal or suspicious person went and how, i.e., by car, etc.

The campus law enforcement department may also be helpful in providing training for the resident assistants regarding the local laws and ordinances, search and seizure issues, and other legal topics. If the campus has an active crime prevention program, it is very useful to involve the resident assistants as early as possible. This group should receive training relative to crime prevention programs such as: personal safety/rape prevention, bicycle security, property theft prevention, and other programs unique to their environment. After the training is received, the campus law enforcement department should follow-up with the resident assistants as soon as the new students arrive in the residence hall facilities. This serves to reinforce the training which the resident assistants received as well as enhance the overall crime prevention efforts involving as many students as possible.

Crisis Intervention Training For Residence Hall Staff

Residence hall staff members will encounter many students living in their facility who are undergoing difficult periods of transition in their lives. These students will be facing both academic and social difficulties and pressures at various times. Many students will actually experience emotional problems and face a potential crisis during the time they are living in the residence hall. The Counseling Testing Service at the University of Houston has provided the following definition of "crisis." A crisis involves:

1. A person who has conveyed verbally or behaviorally that she/he is a danger to self and/or others;
2. A person who is disoriented and confused or lacks contact with reality;
3. An individual who is experiencing severe stress; or
4. Anyone who physically disrupts university operations.[13]

Once the residence hall staff members have received background information regarding the nature and extent of emotional problems on campuses throughout the country and are aware of how a crisis may be defined, it is important that they receive specific information regarding behaviors which indicate that a potential crisis for a student may be forthcoming. While many students report that they experience periodic problems such as depression or anxiety, feelings of isolation, or other difficulties in adjusting to college life, it is critical that residence hall staff be aware of the following indicators of potential crisis:

1. High or increasing level of stress (feeling overwhelmed);
2. Poor coping ability of the student (as when the person becomes easily frustrated and/or angry);
3. Lacking a good support system of friends, family, and acquaintances (nobody to talk with);

4. A negative attitude or sense of hopelessness about their problem(s); and
5. Reduced social contact and/or "sloppy" appearance.[14]

Should a student's emotional crisis not be properly identified and dealt with, there is the possibility that the student will attempt or commit suicide. While the residence hall staff members are not expected to be fully trained mental health practitioners, it is important that they be provided with specific training regarding signs which indicate the student has a greater potential for suicide. If the residence hall staff member is observant of these behaviors and quickly brings this information to their supervisor, a tragedy may be averted. At that point, a proper referral may be made to the on-campus counseling center or similar community resource. The Counseling and Testing Service at the University of Houston has identified seven signs relating to student behavior which indicate a greater potential for suicide:

1. Early morning awakenings.
2. Having the "morning blues."
3. Little or no interest in activities or conversations.
4. Sudden improvement (indicating they may have decided to take their own life) or initial improvement (which may indicate the student has regained enough energy to *act* upon their suicidal thoughts);
5. Becoming increasingly withdrawn and isolated;
6. Not being able to express how badly they are feeling and "keeping everything inside"; and
7. Not having much remorse or feelings of sorrow about a previous suicide attempt.[15]

ALCOHOL/DRUG SECURITY ISSUES

In society, there is a well-established relationship between alcohol and other drug abuse in crimes committed. Unfortunately, alcohol and drug abuse on our college campuses are also closely related to crimes being committed. It is not unusual to hear of crimes such as disorderly conduct, public intoxication, theft, assaults, and other crimes of personal violence having been associated with alcohol or drug abuse. According to a report recently issued by the U.S. Department of Justice, examples of ways in which drug and alcohol use contributed to crime include stimulating aggressiveness or weakening inhibitions of offenders or motivitating offenders to commit crimes to get money to buy drugs.[16] This same report indicates that drug use is far greater among offenders than among non-offenders, in that prison inmates use alcohol more than their counterparts in the general population. There is clearly a relationship between drug and alcohol use in criminal activity, although it is somewhat unclear as to the strength of that relationship.

The use and abuse of alcohol by students is a particular concern to campus administrators from both an enforcement and liability standpoint. For example, one study indicates that half the assailants in courtship-violence situations were reported to have been drinking.[17] Another report issued by the Dean of Students Department at the Georgia Institute of Technology provides further examples of the increasing threat of health and welfare of college students which alcohol abuse represents.

> During the Fall Quarter, 1983, seven alcohol-related deaths nearly occurred. Four students were treated for lethal doses of alcohol and three students were involved in serious alcohol-related vehicle accidents.
> The Georgia Tech Health Center has come to treat between two to four students for acute alcohol intoxication (semi-comatose) each week.
> Approximately 70 percent of campus disorderly conduct, disruptive behavior, and property distruction at Georgia Tech, and 40 percent of academic failures on a national level are alcohol related.
> The leading cause of death among 18- to 23-year-old populations are alcohol-related accidents, alcohol homicides, and alcohol-related suicides.[18]

Johnson (1987) in a survey of drug/alcohol use among college students also found a high usage of alcohol, marijuana, and cocaine on campus. Other data indicated that:

> Alcohol remained the most widely used substance on college campuses—90.9 percent of the students in 1987.
> Marijuana decreased from 40.9 percent in 1986 to 37.0 percent in 1987, but, according to Johnson, the percentage is still "disturbingly high."
> LSD use slightly increased from 3.9 percent in 1986 to 4.0 percent in 1987.
> Heroin use slightly increased from 0.1 percent in 1986 to 0.2 percent in 1987.
> An overall decrease was observed with all other illicit drugs including opiates, stimulants, sedatives, and tranquilizers.[19]

Campus administrators cannot afford to ignore the use and abuse of illegal drugs and alcohol on their campuses. This information coupled with the clear association between drugs/alcohol and crime create additional security concerns for campus officials. From a liability standpoint, campus administrators are now becoming increasingly aware of individuals seeking compensation for alcohol-related injuries or death. Colleges and universities whose members clearly consume and in many cases serve alcoholic beverages are aware that their institution often plays a role that may allow injured persons to seek damages from the institution. The roles are:

> As supervisor of student conduct;
> As a property owner;
> As a seller of alcohol; and
> As a "social host."[20]

Campus administrators should be aware of case law developments in order to reduce their liability risks as they relate to these roles.

Campus Alcohol Policy

Many campuses have developed policies regarding alcohol which provide guidelines relative to possession, sale, and consumption of alcohol. These guidelines should apply to individuals as well as organized groups of faculty, staff, students, and non-affiliates who are guests of same. The policy should discourage alcohol abuse and make it very clear that alcohol at on-campus events is to be served as an amenity to the activity and not an essential element of it. The policy should underscore and comply with local ordinances and appropriate state laws. It should disallow individuals to bring their own alcoholic beverage to an on-campus event. Non-affiliated guests should be designated as the responsibility of the student, faculty, or staff member they are accompanied by. It should be a requirement that food be served at any on-campus event where alcohol is served as well as serving an equal amount of non-alcoholic beverages. The policy should clearly designate what will be considered an acceptable form of identification, such as driver's license, passport, or military identification, each of which includes a photograph of the individual.

Prior to an event being scheduled on campus wherein alcohol is served or allowed to be consumed, there should be an event approval process. Many campuses have established committees to review requests for events where alcohol will be served. Frequently, members of the

Student Affairs Office, student organizations, campus law enforcement, the safety officer, and other appropriate personnel are included on the approval committee. Before the event is approved, it should be clearly established the type of alcohol that will be served, the number of people anticipated to be at the event, the number of people at the event who will be below the legal age of alcohol consumption, what pre-event advertising will be approved (again the advertising should make it clear that alcohol is the amenity and not the purpose of the event), provide for security at the event, and designate who is responsible for event cleanup.

If it is a student organization requesting event approval, that organization's student advisor should be present at the event-approval meeting. The student advisor will play a key role in making sure that all members of the organization are aware of the campuses' policy. Campus administrators should consider restricting areas in which alcoholic beverages may be possessed and/or consumed. The organization's student advisor should play an active role in ensuring compliance with all pre-event stipulations.

Some colleges and universities have gone well beyond developing policies and procedures regarding drugs or alcohol use/abuse. Many colleges have developed staff training programs on topics such as: recognizing behaviors associated with alcohol/drug abuse, identification of illegal drugs, search and seizure issues, applicable local and state laws, campus policies and procedures regarding drugs and alcohol, and how, when, and where to make appropriate referrals of students, faculty, and staff exhibiting abuse problems.

Campuses have also initiated proactive public education programs to make all who live and work in the campus setting fully aware of the extent of the problems involved. These programs typically include distribution of any policies or procedures relative to drug and alcohol abuse. Frequently, the public education program will be made a part of new student and employee orientation and even included in certain academic courses. It is also important that during this education program, counseling resources and the proper referral processes to those programs be identified. Early intervention by professional counselors may very well reduce the chances for a crisis occurring in the future. The campuses' disciplinary sanctions for violating these policies and/or the judicial ramifications for violating ordinances or law should be made apparent and discussed in the education programs. Rutgers University has developed a number of programs to deal with alcohol abuse on their campus. They are highlighted as follows:

Alcohol education—Rutgers' students who have been trained and supervised by professional, conduct workshops on drug and alcohol use upon request from fraternities, sororities, clubs, classes, and residence hall groups.

Alcohol assistance—This rehabilitation program, begun in 1983, is run by certified alcohol counselors. Its aim is to treat those in recovery from alcoholism or other substance abuse. Services include individual and group counseling and follow-up.

Support groups—There are campus support groups for recovering people as well as the children of alcoholics. Rutgers has actually set aside part of an apartment complex for people in recovery.

Inpatient substance abuse clinic—An inpatient clinic with beds set aside for 15 students with substance abuse problems is now located at Rutgers. The program, run by professional personnel, has several components including detoxification and intensive individual and group therapy.[21]

Drug-free Work Place

Many colleges and universities which receive federal assistance are now seeking to comply with federal law in order to make their work settings drug free. These campuses are attempting to ensure that all their campus personnel understand the proper procedures to be followed as they relate to the unlawful manufacture, distribution, dispensation, possession, or use of controlled substances in the work place. A sample of one such statement of policy is as follows:

The unlawful manufacture, distribution, dispensation, possession, or use of a controlled substance is prohibited in and on the campus's owned or controlled property. Any campus employee determined to have violated this policy shall be subject to disciplinary action for misconduct, which action may include termination. No employee is to report to work while under the influence of illegal drugs. Violation of these policies by an employee will be reason for evaluation/treatment for a drug use disorder and for disciplinary action to up and including termination in accordance with applicable collective bargaining agreements, policies, and procedures.

In order to comply with federal law, the campus requires that an employee notify the employer of any criminal drug statute conviction for a violation occurring in the work place no later than five days after such a conviction. The campus must notify any federal contracting agency within ten days of having received notice that an employee engaged in the performance of such contract or grant has a criminal drug statute conviction for a violation occurring in the work place. The campus will discipline any employee who is so convicted or require the employee's satisfactory participation in a drug abuse assistance or reha-bilitation program.[22]

Campuses may also choose to include information in their educational brochures and other publications which will help students and other members of the campus environment to understand the impact of illegal drugs. The following are actual scenarios of incidents that have occurred which appear in a public education brochure distributed by the campus police department at Massachusetts Institute of Technology:

> The student who collected funds from a group arranged to make a buy involving several hundred dollars. At the meeting, the smiling pusher had a switchblade resulting in loss of money with no drugs delivered.
>
> A "friend" from another university who dropped by the dorm to deliver some pot, made mental notes and observations of the surroundings. Later, while the residents were at class, the subject returned with friends. Result: loss of stereo equipment, radio, camera, jewelry, etc.
>
> A student unsuspectingly makes a buy at Harvard Square from an undercover narcotics agent who follows the trail back to the dorm. Surveillance of the dorm results in two arrests and criminal records for two students.
>
> Peer pressure. A, using acid (LSD) with no bad trips, convinces B he doesn't know what he is missing. B has a bad reaction, cannot be restrained, takes clothes off to go outside and run in traffic and is injured. Three weeks later, B suffers unprovoked reoccurrence of bad trip, is hospitalized for weeks and blows a semester. A still cannot understand it.
>
> Semester scene: You learned to handle it in high school—good Acapulco Gold. Now you're on your own. Schedule? Monday, mind, pot, drifting and dreaming; Tuesday, music and euphoria; Wednesday, dreaming and drifting; Thursday, potheads unite! Friday, who needs 18.01? Let's do it again. Repeat next week. Result: loss of initiative, withdrawal, fade out, dropout of MIT.[23]

SUGGESTED SECURITY QUESTIONS

1. Is the campus law enforcement department involved in the training of residence hall staff members concerning their role in safety and security issues?
2. Are residence hall staff members aware of the responsibilities and legal authority of the campus law enforcement department?
3. Do the residence hall department and the campus law enforcement

department have a written policy outlining the basic responsibilities of both units?

4. Has the campus administration considered forming a crisis response team to be comprised of representatives from student life, health services, the campus counseling center, and the campus law enforcement department?
5. How frequently are dorms reviewed from a security standpoint?
6. Does the security review of residence halls include physical security items such as locks, lights, and shrubbery?
7. Does the campus routinely sponsor special events which will require the presence of campus law enforcement officials?
8. Did the campus experience crimes of violence at the site of special events held within the last year?
9. If the campus did experience property crimes or crimes of violence at special events, how does that number compare with preceding years?
10. Does the campus have an alcohol possession and consumption policy?
11. If the campus does have an alcohol possession and consumption policy, how is it enforced?
12. Does the campus have an illegal drug policy?
13. Does the campus have a pre-event approval policy before special events can be scheduled?
14. If the campus does have a pre-event approval policy, are members of the campus law enforcement department, safety office, and student life office made a part of the pre-event approval process?
15. Does the campus maintain records regarding the number of students treated for mental health or other emotional problems?
16. What is the number of students receiving professional assistance for emotional problems during the last 12 months?
17. Have persons such as the campus law enforcement officers, student counselors, residence hall staff been specifically trained in how to respond to mental health emergencies?
18. Is there a policy on campus regarding how to respond to students or other campus members who exhibit mental health or emotional problems?
19. If a student or other campus community member exhibits behaviors which indicate they might be a threat to themselves or others, does the campus have a 24-hour-a-day intervention service available to all members of the college community?

20. Which department on campus has primary responsibility for fire safety?
21. Regarding fire safety issues, have the specific responsibilities of departments such as student residence halls, campus law enforcement, and physical plant department been clearly identified?
22. Does the campus have concise policies relating to fire safety which are consistent with the educational mission of the institution?
23. Are fire safety policies routinely distributed throughout the campus?
24. Are fire safety education programs routinely offered to key members of the campus such as residence hall staff, physical plant, and campus law enforcement?
25. Are campus fire extinguishers inspected frequently and according to schedule?
26. Does the campus safety office have an established schedule of fire safety inspections for campus facilities?
27. Are fire safety and evacuation training sessions held for campus student residents and employees?
28. Does the campus hold unannounced fire drills in the student residence halls and academic buildings?
29. Has the campus established disciplinary sanctions for those persons found guilty of inappropriate use of fire safety equipment such as extinguishers or alarms?
30. Does the campus have a fire safety committee comprised of students, faculty, and staff which provide input on policy matters in this area?

ENDNOTES

1. Raddatz, Anita. *Crime on Campus: Institutional Tort Liability for the Criminal Acts of Third Parties.* Washington, D.C.: National Association of College and University Attorneys, 1989, p. 18.
2. Ibid., p. 19.
3. Dasch, Larry G. "Campus Residence Halls—An Approach to Initiating a Comprehensive Security Program." *Campus Law Enforcement Journal,* Jan.–Feb.: 14, 1989.
4. "Dorm Security and College Liability." In Leonard Territo and Max L. Bromley (Eds.), *Hospital and College Security Liability.* Columbia, MD: Hanrow Press, 1987, p. 171.
5. *Vandalism Who Loses.* Pennsylvania State University, Department of University Safety, State College, Pennsylvania, 1988.

6. *Police Division Multi-Topic Safety Awareness Pamphlet.* Michigan State University Department of Public Safety, East Lansing, Michigan, 1988, pp. 3, 4.

7. Ibid., p. 10.

8. *Fire Safety in Residence Halls.* Northwestern University Department of Public Safety, Evanston, IL: 1988, p. 2.

9. *Fire Safety for Residence Hall Staff and House Residents.* Northwestern University, Evanston, IL: 1988, p. 3.

10. *Fire Safety Manual.* University of Georgia Department of Public Safety, Athens, GA.: 1989, p. 3.

11. Ibid., pp. 10, 11.

12. *Residence Life Staff Training Manual.* University of Delaware Public Safety Department, Newark, Delaware, 1987, pp. 4, 5.

13. *Crisis Intervention Protocol.* University of Houston Counseling and Testing Service, Houston, Texas, 1988, p. 22.

14. *How to Spot Students in Trouble.* University of Houston Counseling and Testing Service, Houston, Texas, 1988, p. 3.

15. Ibid., p. 5, 6.

16. *Report to the Nation on Crime and Justice.* U.S. Department of Justice, Washington, D.C.: 1988, p. 50.

17. Bogal-Allbritten, Rosemarie B. and William Allbritten. "The Hidden Victims: Courtship Violence Among College Students." *Journal of College Student Personnel,* May, 1985, p. 201.

18. *Alcohol Policy.* Dean of Students, Georgia Institute of Technology, Atlanta, GA: p. 1.

19. *College Security Report.* Rusting Publications, Port Washington, NY.: p. 1. Readers interested in obtaining more information regarding this study should obtain, *National Trends in Drug Use and Related Factors Among American High School Students and Young Adults, 1975–1986,* published by the National Clearinghouse for Drugs and Alcohol Information, Rockville, MD.

20. *Student Alcohol Abuse and University Liability: Who Will Pay the Price?* In Leonard Territo and Max L. Bromley (Eds.), *Hospital and College Security Liability.* Columbia, MD: Hanrow Press, p. 68.

21. *College Security Report.* Rusting Publications, Port Washington, NY.: p. 7.

22. *Drug-Free Workplace,* University of South Florida, Tampa, FL, p. 1.

23. *Straight Talk About Drugs on Campus: A Guide for the MIT Student,* Massachusetts Institute of Technology Campus Police Department, Cambridge, Massachusetts, 1988, p. 5.

Chapter 4

OFF-CAMPUS APARTMENT SECURITY

For a variety of reasons, many college students choose to live in apartments off the main college campus. In some apartment complexes, the tenants are comprised primarily of students and are considered attractive targets of opportunity for criminals. In such areas, one can too often find a high number of rapes as well as thefts. Anytime there is a large number of young females concentrated in a given area, one can expect it to be an attractive target for potential rapists. In addition, some of these students have expensive stereo systems in their apartments as well as in their automobiles which make them attractive to thieves. Both rapists and thieves are generally opportunists; thus, the more secure one's person and property is, the less attractive they become to potential criminals.

In this chapter, we will suggest a number of practical ways in which apartments can be made more secure and suggest behaviors that reduce the possibility of being victimized.

SECURITY WHEN MOVING INTO AND OUT OF APARTMENTS

Lone females, either moving into or out of an apartment, can be particularly vulnerable. The following case illustrates this point.

> Several years ago in a large southern city, a rapist dubbed "The Suitcase Rapist" by local police was attacking lone females while they were in the process of moving into or out of their apartment complexes. In some cases, the females left their apartments unlocked while returning to their vehicles parked on nearby parking lots. The rapist would then enter the unlocked apartment and wait for the lone female to return. When she returned he would overpower her and rape her.

It is very simple to minimize the chances of becoming a victim of this type of crime. What is needed is for the woman to be certain that the apartment door is locked every time she goes to her vehicle to either deliver or retrieve some of her personal belongings. It is also recommended

73

that the vehicle be locked every time it is unattended in order to protect the contents of the car.

SECURITY OF DOORS

Before someone considers moving into an apartment, they should be certain that the locks have been rekeyed, including the sliding glass doors. This point cannot be overemphasized, since it is impossible to determine if the previous tenants have retained spare keys. One of the authors, while working as a rape squad detective, investigated the rape of a woman who was attacked in her apartment while in bed asleep. There were no signs of any forcible entry into the apartment. The woman insisted that she had locked all of her doors and windows before going to sleep, but the police were skeptical and suspected that she left one or the other unlocked. Several weeks later, when the rapist was arrested in connection with another similar rape, a key to the first victim's apartment was found in the rapist's possession. This key was identified by a member of the rapist's family as belonging to the apartment in which the family had previously lived. The rapist had kept a duplicate key to the apartment when he and his family moved out. The management of the apartment complex did not rekey the lock, thus making it easy for the rapist to enter what the victim believed was a secure apartment.

The representative of the apartment complex should be asked if locks to all apartments are rekeyed when tenants move out, and if not, they should be requested to do so. If they refuse, serious consideration should be given to living elsewhere. If a prospective tenant really likes the apartment in spite of this, then they should go through the personal expense of having the locks rekeyed. The peace of mind will be worth it. However, since most apartment complexes require a duplicate key to all apartments in the event of an emergency, such as a broken water pipe or perhaps even the need to enter for routine maintenance such as changing air conditioning filters and fumigating, the management of the property will probably have to be given an extra key when the locks are rekeyed.

WHAT TYPES OF LOCKS ARE BEST

Unfortunately, too many apartment complexes still use only the key-in-knob type of lock (see Figure 4-1). This particular lock can be easily defeated by the most amateur burglars with a credit card or screwdriver inserted between the latch and the strike plate. The lock offers no security and should be supplemented by a single- or double-cylinder dead bolt lock or rim type or surface-mounted lock. This dead latch is similar to the spring latch lock but has a smaller bar or plunger which will not permit opening with a jimming device. This is a poor security device, since the plunger is very short and weak and should be supplemented by a quality dead bolt. If the door to the apartment does not have a dead bolt lock, one should be installed. However, the tenants of the apartment will quite likely have to receive permission from the apartment manager to do so and, after the lock is installed, provide a duplicate key.[1]

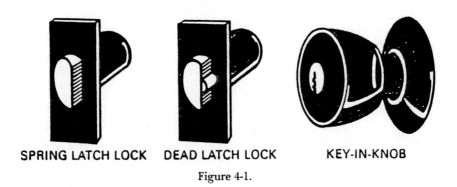

SPRING LATCH LOCK   DEAD LATCH LOCK   KEY-IN-KNOB

Figure 4-1.

An example of a dead bolt lock appears in Figure 4-2 and there are essentially two types. One is referred to as a single-cylinder dead bolt lock which should be mounted on a solid wood core door when there is no breakable glass within 40 inches of the interior locking mechanism. The single-cylinder dead bolt lock has a thumb turn place on the inside. The second type is a double-cylinder dead bolt lock which is key operated from both the interior and exterior and should be used when there is glass within 40 inches of the interior locking mechanism.

Both single- and double-cylinder dead bolt locks should meet certain basic criteria to be considered a good security device. The bolt must be extended a minimum of one inch and must be cased hardened and contain a hard insert to the cylinder guard which must be tapered or spherical in design to make it difficult to grip with pliers or a wrench. It must be made of solid steel, not a hollow casting or stamp metal, and preferably be able to turn freely; the connecting screws that hold the lock

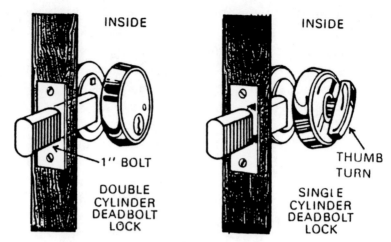

Figure 4-2.

together must both be put on the inside. There must be no exposed screw heads on the exterior of the door; the connecting screws must be at least one-quarter inch in diameter and screw into solid metal stock, not screw posts.

When shopping for a dead bolt lock, one may wish to take the diagram and description in Figure 4-2 to a locksmith or hardware store to be certain the lock that is purchased will meet all the security requirements. This applies to all locks depicted in this chapter.

However, even when these locks are installed, the tenant may be concerned because the key to the apartment is in the hands of the apartment manager and other apartment personnel. There are a number of things that can be done to make the apartment secure, even if there is a possibility that someone employed by the apartment complex may be dishonest. Figure 4-3 provides an illustration of a lock which can neutralize this problem. It should be noted that there is no key to operate the lock from the outside. This means that once the tenant is in the apartment and the latch is turned even if someone has a key to the other door locks, they cannot enter the apartment. However, it must be remembered that this does not provide the tenant with security when out of the apartment, because this lock can only be engaged once a person is in the apartment.

MINIMUM 2" WOOD SCREWS   CARRIAGE BOLTS

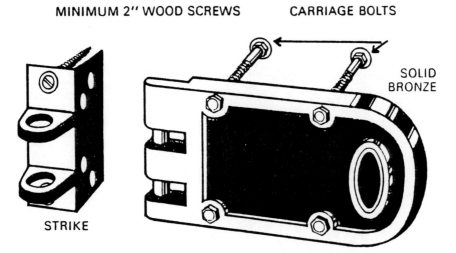

Figure 4-3. Rim type or surface lock (jimmy resistant).

THE VALUE OF A CHAIN LATCH FOR SECURITY

A chain latch offers almost no security at all (see Figure 4-4). Chain latches can be easily ripped off the door with minimum pressure unless they are steel chains attached to steel door frames. If someone should come to the door, the best way to check their identity is to use a wide-angle viewer or peephole (see Figure 4-5). If a wide-angle viewer is not installed in the door, the apartment manager should be requested to do so. If this request is denied, then the tenant should have one installed. Under no circumstances should a tenant have to open the door in order to determine who is at the door. The wide-angle viewer will allow the tenant the opportunity to determine if the person at the front door is who they allege to be. It is wise not to open the door to anyone who does not have business in the apartment.

Sometimes, burglars who have no intention of using force will first try to get into the apartment under some pretext so they can examine the apartment to determine if there are valuables and also study the locks, windows and other means of entry. Repairmen, and others who claim to have business inside, should be asked to provide identification. If the tenant has the slightest doubt about the authenticity of the person at their front door, the worker's superiors should be telephoned. The telephone number should be retrieved from the local directory and not

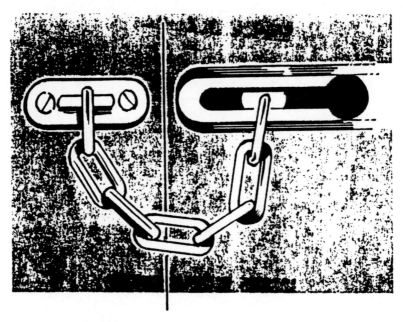

Figure 4-4. Chain latch (of little value).

be requested of the individual who is at the front door. If a tenant wishes to help a stranded motorist or a lost deliveryman, they can make the phone call while the person waits outside. When a workman or a salesperson who is expected is admitted, they should not be left alone at any time.

WINDOW SECURITY

Windows are among the most vulnerable points in an apartment. Apartments which are located on the second or higher floor, especially if there are no fire escapes, ladders or trees which can be climbed lending access to windows, tend to be somewhat less vulnerable than ground-floor windows. There are a number of locking devices that can be installed on windows to make them less vulnerable and most are available at local hardware stores (see Figure 4-6). There is a tendency for people who have become accustomed over the years to sleeping with their bedroom windows open to fail to realize that once they have left the safety and security of their small community and ventured into more concentrated urban areas that this is a luxury they can no longer afford. Windows simply cannot be left open and/or unlocked, especially if they are on the ground floor.

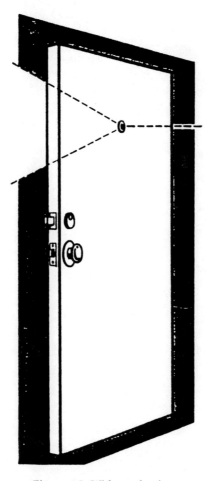

Figure 4-5. Wide-angle viewer.

SLIDING GLASS DOORS

Sliding glass doors present a major security problem if they do not have the proper lock and if special steps are not taken to prevent removal of the door. The sliding glass door is lifted into position when installed and, therefore, must be lifted from the track to be removed. To prevent this, it is recommended that a one-and-one-quarter-inch pan head (large head) sheet metal screw be inserted into the top of the door frame at both ends and middle. These screws should be adjusted so that the door barely clears them when it is operated. In addition, a dowel stick can also be installed in order to prevent the door from being forced open. There

DOUBLE HUNG WINDOW

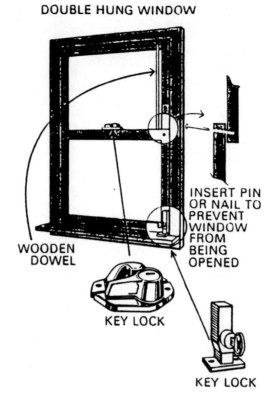

WOODEN DOWEL

INSERT PIN OR NAIL TO PREVENT WINDOW FROM BEING OPENED

KEY LOCK

KEY LOCK

Figure 4-6.

are also numerous supplementary locks that can be added in addition to the one installed by the manufacturer. It must be remembered that if the sliding glass door is locked with a key, it too must be rekeyed.

SELECTING A ROOMMATE

Selecting the right roommate can be as important as having the right kind of security in an apartment. The following story told to one of the authors by a college coed illustrates this point. She said that she was very safety conscious and had done everything possible to make her off-campus apartment safe, including the installation of special locks on the doors and windows. However, she had a roommate who would frequently go to class in the morning before she woke up and would leave the door to the apartment unlocked. This roommate would also leave the bedroom windows open at night while she slept and their apartment was

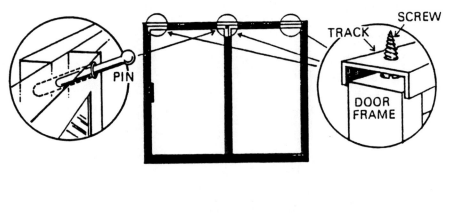

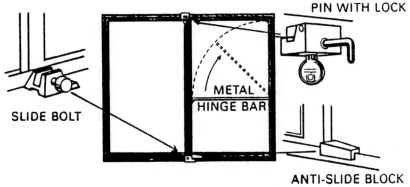

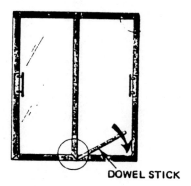

Figure 4-7.

on the ground floor. In spite of her constant efforts to have her roommate become more sensitive to the increased potential for their both becoming victims of a crime because of her actions, the roommate simply ignored her. When asked what she should do, one of the authors advised her to find a new roommate because it is very difficult, if not impossible, to convince a young, naive person that their behavior somehow threatens their well-being and the well-being of others. It is unfortunate, but by the time such persons finally learn the lesson, if ever, the damage may have already been done. Therefore, it is absolutely imperative that one be very careful in selecting a roommate.

Problems can also result when young women fail to close their drapes, blinds, shades and other devices when disrobing. In a case investigated by one of the authors, two young women were sharing an off-campus apartment. One of the women regularly disrobed in front of her window without being certain that her drapes were completely pulled shut. One day, when this particular roommate was gone, the apartment was broken into and the more conscientious roommate was raped. The rapist was eventually arrested and confessed that the attraction to the apartment was the female whom he had seen disrobe herself in front of her window on several occasions. He decided to break into the apartment to rape her, but once he forcibly entered the apartment and found she was gone, he simply seized upon the opportunity to rape the other roommate who was in bed asleep.

CHECKING ON APARTMENT COMPLEX EMPLOYEES

The apartment complex management staff should be questioned about how they conduct pre-employment checks of their employees. It makes no sense to have the finest security systems in the world if they employ people whose backgrounds are questionable or if they fail to conduct proper background inquiries on their employees. Prospective tenants should ask the apartment complex representative to explain what efforts they have made to check out their employees. For example, do they conduct background investigations, do they administer polygraph examinations, and so forth.

LIGHTING

There is little question that exterior lighting in and about the apartment complex can serve as a considerable crime deterrent. The average person looking for an apartment will typically visit the apartment complex during the daytime which is when normal business hours are conducted by the rental office. However, it might be wise to go back to the facility during the evening hours just to see how well lit the area is. This includes the parking lot and walkways leading to the apartment as well as the area to the apartment entrance. If the lighting is poor, it can provide an opportunity for the would-be criminal to conceal himself. The evaluation of the lighting should include checking along the sides of the building as well as the front of the building. Since would-be rapists and thieves are opportunists, it generally means that they have to hang around an area for enough time to find a potential victim to rape or to case an apartment to burglarize later on. Good lighting discourages this type of loitering.

SHRUBBERY

The same rules apply for shrubbery as they do for lighting. Although shrubbery certainly adds an attractive and aesthetic feature to the apartment complex, it may also provide places of concealment for would-be assailants. Once again, it is best to check out the facility during the evening hours to see if, in fact, the shrubbery allows places of concealment. This is especially true if the shrubbery provides places of concealment up against the building near ground-floor windows.

EMPLOYMENT OF SECURITY PERSONNEL

Most apartment complexes do not employ security personnel. However, those that do frequently confine their activities to the evening hours. It should be ascertained from the apartment complex representative if they have security personnel on duty and, if so, the areas they patrol and the number of hours they are on duty. It may be that an apartment complex has employed a single security guard to patrol an enormous complex which makes the presence of that person of limited value. Efforts should be made to determine if the security guard is trained and also if that person is in two-way radio communication with some main station that can summon assistance if needed.

SECURITY OF PERSONAL VEHICLES

The breaking and entering of automobiles on the parking lots of apartment complexes is becoming increasingly more common. Typically, the targets of opportunity are expensive stereo equipment, tape decks and, in some cases, car telephones. There are a number of things which can make the vehicle a less attractive target to the would-be thief. First, to begin with, if the opportunity presents itself one should park in the most lighted area of the parking lot. Second, if valuables such as purses, wallets, credit cards, jewelry or weapons must be left in the car, they should not be left in the passenger compartment or the glove compartment of the car. They should be locked in the trunk of the car. More often than not, burglars will not force their way into the trunk of the car, but they will force their way into the passenger compartment and glove compartment. If the vehicle is equipped with expensive stereo equipment that would be attractive to would-be thieves, it would be wise to install a car alarm if one can be afforded. In lieu of this option, it might be wise to advise any security personnel on duty at the complex to keep a special watch on the car.

YOUR NAME CAN SAY TOO MUCH

Placing an entire name on a mailbox gives would-be criminals an unnecessary advantage. For example, it tells anyone who wants to know that the apartment is occupied by a woman living alone. Figure 4-8 provides an example of the do's and don'ts of mailbox identification.

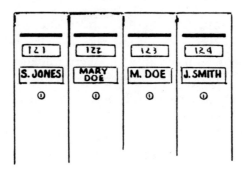

Figure 4-8.

SECURITY OF KEYS

The finest locks in the world are of little value if some unauthorized person has access to the keys. Keys should not be hidden under doormats or in other places where they may be easily found. If someone is concerned about accidentally locking themselves out of their apartment, they can give a duplicate key to a trusted friend or neighbor. Car keys and house keys should be on a key ring or other device which allows them to be separated. For example, if a car needs to be left for repairs, only the ignition key should be left behind. Even if the car is taken to a full-service car wash and the driver is required to exit, only the ignition key should be left in the car.

Neither a name nor apartment number should appear on one's key ring (see Figure 4-9). If they are lost, someone could use them to enter one's home or apartment. If the keys are lost and especially if they are lost away from the immediate area where one works or lives, it is highly unlikely anyone would be able to identify them as belonging to a specific person. However, if it is suspected that they may have been stolen from a purse or from any other location which would link them to a specific person, then the locks must be rekeyed immediately.

Correct   Incorrect

Figure 4-9.

OTHER SECURITY SUGGESTIONS FOR SAFE APARTMENT LIVING

1. Always respond to the door bell or the phone, otherwise a potential burglar may think the apartment is unoccupied and break in. When the door is answered, the tenant should never let the caller know that only one person is at home. The impression should be given that someone else is in the house.

2. In the case of unexpected service and repairmen, verify their identities and purposes with their employers before you open the door. If a decision is made to allow them to enter the apartment, arrangements should be made to have either a friend or neighbor there or have someone monitor the tenant with periodic phone calls. Make these precautions obvious.

3. If someone the tenant does not fully trust asks to make an emergency phone call, the door should not be opened. The call can be made for them.

4. Care should be taken when giving out information concerning oneself or where one lives, either in person, by mail or over the phone.

5. Keep emergency phone numbers posted on phones.

6. When returning home, the tenant should make sure that she is not being followed and should be alert for anyone who may be waiting for her to unlock her door so that they can force their way into her apartment. She should have her keys ready before she gets to her door.

7. If, when returning home, she has reason to believe that an unauthorized entry has been made, she should not enter her apartment but instead go to a safe place immediately, such as a neighbor's house, and get help before she attempts to enter.

8. The tenant should plan her fastest escape routes out of her apartment in case she ever has to exit quickly.

9. If she finds herself trapped in her apartment by an intruder and she must yell for help, she may want to yell "Fire!" This will often get a better response. She should not hesitate to throw something through a window or cause noise in any other way that might bring attention to her plight.

10. Lone women should be especially cautious of laundry rooms, parking lots or any other isolated area. Apartment tenants should insist that these areas be well lit and try to use these areas only in the company of other trusted individuals.[2]

SUGGESTED APARTMENT SECURITY QUESTIONS

Students who are looking for off-campus apartments should ask the apartment complex representatives the following questions:

1. Does the management of the apartment routinely rekey all locks once the apartment is vacated?
2. Do apartment doors have dead bolt locks?
3. Do the doors of the apartments have a wide-angle viewer thus eliminating having to open the door to see who is there?
4. Are any supplementary locks installed on the apartment windows?
5. Are there supplementary locks on the sliding glass doors?
6. Has every possible effort been made to find out if a prospective roommate is safety conscious and has a compatible life-style and habits?
7. How does the management of the apartment complex go about checking their employees, i.e., do they conduct background investigations or administer polygraph examinations?
8. Is the apartment complex well lit? This includes the parking lots, sides of the building, back of the buildings, walkways to apartments and the areas around the entryway to apartments.
9. Is shrubbery cut back so that it does not provide places of concealment for potential assailants or burglars?
10. Does the apartment complex employ security personnel? If so, are they trained, how many security personnel do they have on duty and what times are they on duty?
11. If security personnel are employed, are they in two-way radio communication with a main station?
12. If there is expensive stereo equipment in one's vehicle and security personnel are employed, have they been specifically requested to keep an eye on the car?
13. Has the apartment complex management been requested to provide information about the number of burglaries, auto thefts, burglaries of autos, and rapes that have occurred in the apartment complex over the past couple of years?
14. Are laundry rooms located in an area where they are visible to passersby?

ENDNOTES

1. *Residential Burglary,* Office of the Attorney General, Tallahassee, Florida, 1978. Much of this discussion of locks and accompanying figures were adapted from this source.
2. *Sexual Assault Prevention.* The North Carolina Crime Prevention Division, Department of Crime Control and Public Safety, Raleigh, North Carolina, 1988, pp. 4 and 5.

Chapter 5

PREVENTING RAPES

According to the 1988 FBI figures, there were 227 rapes on college campuses. It is pretty well accepted that rapes of all types are rarely reported, and it is estimated that only 10 percent of all rapes come to the attention of the police. Thus, if these figures are accurate, then many more thousands of rapes are occurring on college campuses every year that never come to the attention of the police. The reasons most often cited by women for not reporting these rapes are as follows:

1. Lack of belief in the ability of the police to apprehend the suspect.
2. Concern that they would receive unsympathetic treatment from the police and would have to go through discomforting procedures.
3. Desire to avoid the embarrassment of publicity.
4. Fear of reprisal by the rapist.
5. Apprehension based on television programs or newspaper reports that they would be further victimized by court proceedings.[1]
6. Fear that parents would make them leave school.

In this chapter, we will provide information and suggestions which, if adhered to, will greatly minimize the possibility of a student becoming the victim of a rape. We will examine some of the myths associated with rape and the preventive measures most effective in protecting oneself against stranger-to-stranger rapes, acquaintance rape, and gang rape.

MYTH VS. REALITY

We are conditioned to certain concepts about sexual assault—others are learned later. The reader should compare his or her perceptions with the following myths and realities:

Myth. Rape usually happens at night and in dark places.

Reality. Rape can occur anytime, anywhere. Reports give evidence of a variety of settings: inside buildings, parking lots, alleys, garages, parks, campuses, and in the victim's home.

Myth. The rapist attacks to feed sexual desires.

89

Reality. This is a widespread misconception. Most rapists already have normal channels for sexual gratification. In general, a rapist is very insecure and frustrated at his lack of control. Rape provides a temporary non-sexual fulfillment of domination and humiliation. Sex is used as a tool to invade the victim's valued privacy and to invoke a feeling of power that is normally lacking.

Myth. Attacks are spontaneous.

Reality. Some attacks are premeditated. The rapist may have planned the attack for only an hour or for weeks.

Myth. Rapists come from the "wrong side of the tracks"; they are low on the socioeconomic scale.

Reality. Not every rapist fits this description. The rapist may be a good-looking, well-educated, financially successful person.

Myth. Many rapes are interracial.

Reality. In the majority of reported rapes, the assailant and victim are of the same race.

Myth. Most rapists are not known by their victims.

Reality. In many of the reported rapes, the rapist is no stranger. The rapist is an acquaintance, a coworker, a classmate, a relative, or a neighbor.

Myth. "Flashers," "peeping toms," and obscene phone callers are perfectly harmless.

Reality. No one knows. Some commit only these "nuisance" offenses for years without ever progressing to assault. Others, though, may progress to more serious offenses.

Myth. Victims who wore sexy outfits or behaved flirtatiously "asked for it."

Reality. No one ever "asks" for violence by their dress or flirting manner.

Myth. Good-looking people are more likely to be chosen as victims.

Reality. Victims range from 6 months to 90 years old.

Myth. Women have rape fantasies and secretly desire to be raped.

Reality. Females and males may have sexual fantasies, but the characters and action of fantasy are controlled by the dreamer—the reality of rape is not the equivalent of fantasy. The overwhelming majority of women do not secretly desire to be raped.

Myth. People falsely yell "rape" just to get attention.

Reality. As with other crimes, very few people give false reports on rape. On the contrary, nationally more rapes occur than are reported.

Myth. It's your word against his.

Reality. The crime of rape is not that simple. You may not be aware of the legal significance of physical and other evidence. If you are not sure of your circumstances, check with the campus security department.[2]

WHO IS THE RAPIST?

The rapist, in the main, is a man who is emotionally unstable yet deals with life on a day-to-day basis in a reasonably normal and competent manner. In fact, he is often an apparently normal individual but one who has difficulty relating to others in a permanent or lasting fashion, and, according to the reported cases of sexual assault, the assailant is often a friend, date, relative, coworker or casual acquaintance. It is important to remember, too, that exhibitionists and "peeping toms" should be considered as potentially dangerous, since these acts may be only a part of a fantasy which includes rape.

WHY DOES THIS CRIME OCCUR?

It cannot be emphasized too strongly that sexual assault is a crime of violence; that rapists are emotionally unstable persons; that rapists view their victims as objects upon which to vent their hostility, aggression, frustration or insecurity. They obviously do not view their victim as a human being at that moment, and sexual gratification is not a motive for their crime.

They wish to humiliate and degrade their victims, to make them lesser beings than they are, and, too often, the fantasy which they are acting out carries with it the danger of physical harm in addition to the act of rape itself.

WHERE DO SEXUAL ASSAULTS OCCUR ON CAMPUSES?

They can occur virtually anywhere, but the following are the most common areas:

- dormitories (rooms, restrooms and showers)
- parking lots and garages
- laundromats
- classrooms
- stairwells

- hallways
- business offices
- walkways

SELF-PROTECTION IN THE CAR

1. Whenever possible, park in a well-lighted area.
2. One's car should always be locked.
3. A woman should always have her car keys in her hand when walking to her car.
4. If working late, she should try to have a friend or security guard accompany her to her car.
5. Before getting in her car, she should be certain to check the floor of the back seat.
6. When driving, she should keep her car doors locked.
7. If she thinks she's being followed, she should not drive home but instead drive to the nearest gas, fire or police station or to the nearest well-lighted area where there are people.
8. If she has car trouble on the road, she should raise the hood and then wait inside the car with the doors locked and the windows up. If a motorist stops to help, she can crack her window slightly and ask the person to call the police.
9. If she wants to help someone in a disabled vehicle, she should not get out of her car but rather drive to the nearest well-lighted area with a phone and call the police.
10. She should not under any circumstances pick up hitchhikers.
11. She should not pull over for flashing headlights. If it is an emergency vehicle or the police, there will be flashing red or blue lights.[3]

SELF-PROTECTION ON CAMPUS

1. The rapist is looking for a woman who appears vulnerable . . . one who is apparently inattentive to her surroundings, one who is daydreaming or looks frightened and unsure of herself. So, she should keep alert and walk with a purpose. However, she should also keep in mind the fact that there exists a fine line between presenting an air of confidence and what the potentail rapist might perceive as "cockiness." This is where she must use her common sense for a "cocky" attitude or posture, which may cause the potential rapist to "want to pull her down off her pedestal,"

down to his level. The thing to remember is to display enough concern with herself so that she does not appear to be a vulnerable target.

2. If she is being harassed from a vehicle, she should turn and walk in the opposite direction. She should try to head for lights and people. In order to continue the harrassment, the vehicle will have to turn around to follow her.

3. Women should not stop to give directions to a driver or pedestrian. However, if she feels she must, she should maintain enough distance to prevent from being grabbed and dragged into the car or into an isolated area.

4. If she thinks that she is being followed, she should immediately head for the nearest area where there are lights and people.

5. Women should not hitchhike or accept rides from strangers. It is more than risky. It is dangerous. Some rapists use their cars as a way to get a woman alone, and once she is in the car, she has lost control of the situation.

6. If she plans to do some walking, it only makes sense to wear clothing and footwear that give ease and freedom of movement.

INDIVIDUAL REACTIONS

No one knows how a woman will react when actually confronted with the threat of sexual assault. It is a crisis condition. It is an individual response condition, based on strong interacting factors.

She will be able to handle such a situation better if she has a complete awareness and understanding not only of all the dangers inherent in a potential rape situation but of the alternative preventive and tactical measures that she can take as well.

Every woman is a special individual whose attitudes and reactions are the result of a combination of many factors—family life, religious convictions, social interaction with others, basic personality traits and physical condition.

The complexity of the problem of sexual assault is such that she will never really know exactly how she would handle such a situation. This will all depend on what the circumstances are, who she perceives her attacker to be and what her basic personality is.

Since she cannot know what the circumstances might be or who her assailant might be, it is of utmost importance for her to think about who she is and how she would respond to different situations before they occur.

- It may be of prime importance to her to come away with the least possible physical injury.
- She may fear the actual rape more than she fears physical injury.
- The very thought of being sexually assaulted may make her so angry that she would rather face the risk of serious injury.
- She might be more concerned about the safety of a member of her family or a close friend in this situation than she is of either rape or injury.
- The way she reacts may depend on her physical condition.

The list of "ways and whys" of her reaction is infinite and, for this reason, it is important that she understands the different alternatives or tactics on how she could best cope with a rape situation. However, first she needs to know some additional things about rapists in general.

THE ASSAILANT

As mentioned previously, the rapist is an emotionally unstable individual who is using the woman as an object on which to vent his aggression and hostility, and rape is not perpetrated for sexual gratification. It is the use of force, not the sex act itself, that seems to relieve the tension within the rapist and satisfy him. He wants to degrade and humiliate the victim. Sometimes he sees women as being on a pedestal and through the sexual assault he feels he is "cutting them down to size."

The woman does not provoke the attack. It is his problem with which she is dealing and which has become an invasion of her well-being. An attempt should be made to reach him as a human being so that she seems less of an object to him.

Moreover, it should be understood that the rapist does not understand or recognize the rights of an individual. Rapists are opportunists and they look for what they perceive to be vulnerable targets. All rapists have the potential to be violent. This would be a most important consideration when determining alternatives to choose in any given situation.

ALTERNATIVE TACTICS TO USE IF ATTACKED

No one can tell a woman what specific tactic to use, for what may have worked for one woman may not work for another. She must deal with the rapist as an individual. Moreover, she must also take into consideration the time and place, for these, too, will have a bearing on her reaction. Panic and fear are perfectly normal reactions. Also, she should know what the alternative tactics are and what their positive and negative factors are so that she will have the knowledge and awareness necessary to handle the situation in a manner which is most likely to avert the sexual assault.

A Diverting Noise

This is probably a better tactic to use when she has some advance warning of a situation. It is only useful if there is someone nearby to hear the noise and is willing to come to her aid or frighten off the assailant.

Sometimes screaming "Fire" or "Call the police" (not "Rape" or "Help") or blowing a whistle which she has readily available may frighten away the assailant and call attention to her problem. But it may also antagonize him. Screaming could make him angrier and he may beat her or strangle her to keep her quiet. She must weigh the odds, depending on the situation, of this tactic being successful.

Running

The risk with this tactic is whether he can and will run faster than she can and overpower her. Unless she is reasonably certain she can get a good lead and reach safety before he overtakes her, this may be a risky tactic.

She must be certain to have a place to run where someone will help her. It must be kept in mind that running from him may be part of his fantasy and it may make him angrier should he overtake her.

Gaining A Psychological Advantage

Panic and fear are perfectly normal responses. However, if she has mentally prepared herself (in advance) by accepting the fact that she could someday find herself in a rape situation and have thought about what she might do, it may decrease the trauma and allow her to react more quickly in coming to grips with the problem.

This is an intermediate tactic when she needs that precious time to get over the initial panic or fear. She should quickly survey her predicament so she can begin to defuse her assailant's anger.

This tactic can take many forms: going limp, hiding her face in order to stick her finger down her throat and cause herself to vomit, making herself belch, even urinating on her attacker. Her own ingenuity is her best guide. Crying might be effective in some instances. It is doing the unexpected convincingly so that he does not become more antagonistic.

It must be remembered that rapists are con artists, so the intended victim has to be extremely believable. Anything that will not threaten or antagonize him while she looks for a way to get out of the situation should keep her from being hurt.

Talking

The first few moments she may be too terrified to utter a sound. That's perfectly normal. But if she has thought in advance about the possibility of sexual assault, the shock will not be as great. The key to this tactic, which can be successful in aborting an attack, is to speak calmly and sincerely as one human being trying to reach out to another human being. She should not beg, plead, cower or make small talk. Many times, this is what the assailant expects to hear and it may antagonize him further.

As to the subject she selects to talk about, it should be something in which she is interested, something about which she can talk comfortably. It could range from her pet, a recent movie she has seen, a book she is reading, even a recent death in the family. The range of subject matter is limitless. The important thing in the use of this tactic is to attempt to relate the feeling that she sees him as a person.

Hopefully, convincing him that she is seeing him as a person instead of some sort of monster will make him perceive her as an individual offering her concern and not as his enemy. She needs to make him see that she is not an object on which to vent his anger.

She should make an effort to reduce his rage by enhancing his ego and try to gain a psychological advantage over him. It is not wise to give a sermon. He may be trying to rape her because he thinks women are too aloof and it would give him great satisfaction to knock a moralizing female down. To his way of thinking, if he can pull her down it raises his self-esteem. That is why it is extremely important for the intended victim to try to reach the assailant in a way which will break his fantasy and allow him to see her as an individual (not an object) with honest feelings and concerns.

If something she says antagonizes him further, she should switch to another topic as quickly and smoothly as she can.

Fighting

When considering this tactic she should keep in mind that all rapists have the potential for inflicting serious harm—they are all potentially violent. This is probably the last tactic to try if all the others have failed. If she starts out by fighting, she will have little or no opportunity to try any other tactic because she has already committed her behavior. If using this tactic, she must be willing and able to inflict serious injury on her assailant. Surprise and speed of reaction should be used to her benefit. If she uses a fighting tactic which does not completely incapacitate him, she is probably going to be in worse shape. If she tries to fight him and he has a weapon, she must always assume that he will not hesitate to use it.

The risks of being seriously injured by her assailant are greatly increased when using such tactics as biting, scratching, pounding his chest with her fists, trying to spray mace or hair spray into his eyes or using any other weapon which will not completely incapacitate him.

Even victims with extensive training in martial arts are not always successful with quick chops or kicks to vital spots on the body. The struggle itself could arouse or further enrage the assailant.

The victim must remember that if she is going to fight her attacker, she must use surprise and speed to her advantage. For instance, she can gently put her hands on the assailant's face and get her thumbs near his eyes, then press his eyeballs suddenly with her thumbs as hard as she can. This will put the assailant into shock and could blind him. Or she can grab his testicles (not his penis, since it will not be effective), squeeze as hard as she can and jerk or pull to inflict immobilizing pain.

Both of these tactics can be accomplished in such a way so that the assailant is not aware of the intended victim's plans for a physical attack. If used, they must be sure and quick and she must be willing to follow through to ensure the disabling injury of the assailant.

ACQUAINTANCE RAPE

Acquaintance rape, sometimes called date rape, is forced, manipulated or coerced sexual intercourse by a man who is known to the victim.

Acquaintance rape occurs all over the country within all socioeconomic and age groups. However, most victims are women between the
ages of 15 and 24.

The following two examples represent the views of the perpetrator of
the assault and his victim.

> Andy: I really liked Jenny. She would hang around after class and
> talk with me almost every day, so I decided to invite her over to my
> dorm one night and she accepted my invitation. Then when we got into
> my room I made a pass at her; she turned me down. I kind of expected
> that, since most girls say "no" even if they really don't mean it. She was
> really flirting with me and sort of leading me on, so I kept trying to
> make it with her. When she started to struggle, I figured it was just an
> act, so I used a little more force and had sex with her. After all, if she
> didn't want to see me, then why did she come over? Andy has commit-
> ted a crime.
>
> Jenny: Andy and I shared some classes and I thought he was a really
> nice guy. We both enjoyed the same kind of music and when he invited
> me over to his dorm room to listen to a new CD, well ... I thought it
> would be okay. I saw him nearly every day in classes.
>
> I never thought he would attack me. When he started making a pass
> at me I told him "no." I said I just wanted to be friends. But he wouldn't
> listen to me. He just got angry. I tried to resist him, but he was just too
> strong. I never thought he would rape me.

More Facts About Acquaintance Rape:

Most acquaintance rapes are not reported and according to surveys on
acquaintance rape, 90 percent of the victims never report it to the
authorities. Many victims do not associate an attack as a rape when the
rapist is someone they know. In some cases, victims believe they may
have caused the rape by consenting to go out with a man and then getting
caught in a compromising situation. They may find it very difficult to
report the attacker if he had been a friend and may fear that their friends
will think she "led him on" in some way. Some fear their friends may not
believe them at all.

Victims of acquaintance rape tend to feel ashamed, guilty and depressed.
They feel betrayed and lose confidence in their judgment because they
did not recognize the acquaintance as a potential rapist.

Acquaintance rape often results from poor communication. Some men
misunderstand a woman's words and actions and assume that when she
says no, she really means yes. What a person says and how a person
behaves may create conflicting messages. Society has led men and women

to believe that a woman's role is to be passive and a man should be aggressive. Many people feel that a man has a right to be more sexually aggressive when he has dated a woman for a long time, if they have had previous sexual encounters, or if she has "led him on" in some manner. Society further conditions men and women to send strong non-verbal messages about their sexuality by the clothes they wear, the tone of their voice, their body language and eye contact.

What Women Should Know About Acquaintance Rape

- She should communicate clearly what she wants and what her expectations are.
- She should set limits for acceptable sexual behavior.
- She should trust her instincts and learn to express her feelings freely.
- She must learn to be assertive.
- She must learn to say no and mean it.
- She should exercise more caution when dating. On a first date, she should establish the identity of her date and meet at a public place.
- She should continue to exercise caution throughout the dating process and not assume that just because nothing happened on the first date that something won't happen on the second, third or fourth date.
- She must be aware of her surroundings. She can enhance her personal safety by providing her own transportation or making an alternate plan for transportation if her plans suddenly change.
- She must be aware of and responsible for her verbal and non-verbal actions.
- Most acquaintance rapes involve alcohol. She must be aware that alcohol and drugs lower her mental and physical abilities and prevent her from thinking clearly or reacting quickly to potentially dangerous situations.
- When leaving a party, concert or other social event with someone she has just met—no matter how nice he may appear to be—there may be considerable potential for an assault.

What Men Should Know About Acquaintance Rape

- Sexual intercourse without the consent of one's partner constitutes rape and is a crime for which one CAN be arrested and prosecuted. Sexual intercourse with someone who is unable to give consent by being mentally incompetent or unconscious (passed out) constitutes rape as well. There are also various statutes regarding sexual intercourse with a woman under the age of legal consent.

- Men should not assume that because a woman dresses in a "sexy" manner or flirts with you she is seeking a sexual encounter.
- Men should communicate sexual desires clearly and accept and respect a woman's decision when she says no. If she doesn't say yes, he should not assume she means yes.
- Men should not assume that permission for a prior sexual encounter implies that permission also is given for future encounters.
- Men should avoid excessive drugs and alcohol in a dating situation and be responsible for their actions. They should not allow their judgment to become impaired.
- Men should seek education on rape by attending workshops or seminars.[4]

CAMPUS GANG RAPE

The events described below are not isolated or rare occurrences. These experiences—acquaintance gang rape—happen all too frequently at fraternity and/or other campus parties at colleges and universities across the country.

... The 17-year-old freshman woman went to the fraternity "little sister" rush party with two of her roommates. The roommates left early without her. She was trying to get a ride home when a fraternity brother told her he would take her after the party ended. While she waited, two other fraternity members took her into a bedroom to "discuss little sister matters." The door was closed and one of the brothers stood blocking the exit. They told her that in order to become a little sister (an honorary member) she would have to have sex with a fraternity member. She was frightened, fearing they would physically harm her if she refused. She could see no escape. Each of the brothers had sex with her, as did a third who had been hiding in the room. During the next two hours a succession of men went into the room. There were never less than three men with her, sometimes more. After they let her go, a fraternity brother drove her home. He told her not to feel bad about the incident because another woman had also been "upstairs" earlier that night.—(occurred at a large state university)

... It was her first fraternity party. The beer flowed freely and she had much more to drink than she had planned. It was hot and crowded and the party spread out all over the house, so that when three men asked her to go upstairs, she went with them. They took her into a bedroom, locked the door and began to undress her. Groggy with alcohol, her feeble protests were ignored as the three men raped her. When they finished, they put her in the hallway, naked, locking her clothes in the bedroom. —(occurred at a small eastern liberal arts college)

... A 19-year-old woman student was out on a date with her boyfriend and another couple. They were all drinking beer and after going back to the boyfriend's dorm room, they smoked two marijuana cigarettes. The other couple left and the woman and her boyfriend had sex. The woman fell asleep and the next thing she knew she awoke with a man she didn't know on top of her trying to force her into having sex. A witness said the man was in the hall with two other men when the woman's boyfriend came out of his room and invited them to have sex with his unconscious girlfriend. The witness declined to participate, but the other men joined the boyfriend and later, two more men, in raping the woman. —(occurred at a small midwestern college)

... No one was sure how many fraternity brothers had had sex with the young woman the night before. It was at least five, maybe seven or eight. Accounts of the incident differ. The victim, who had been drinking and taking drugs at the party, said that when she asked for a place to sleep the brothers carried her upstairs. She remembers having sex with one of them willingly. Then, one by one, a group of men had sex with her. She pleaded throughout to be left alone. The men insist that she was sober, alert and willing, actually encouraging them. —(occurred at an Ivy League institution)[5]

In the last few years fraternities have enjoyed a resurgence in popularity, and many people speculate that this has occurred because of a swing towards conservatism generally among young people. Fraternities seem to offer young men structure, friendship, formality, and ritual at a time in their lives when they are looking for just such guidance. They also appeal to some men because they provide an intimate atmosphere in the somewhat impersonal setting of many institutions.

The fraternity system on campus brings with it advantages and disadvantages for students and the institution as a whole. Fraternity members point to the encouragement given them in study habits, social service projects and organizational development. Some fraternities perform worthwhile public services such as tutorial services, "big brother" programs, and so forth. On the other hand, many believe that these positive activities and programs can be achieved outside the fraternity framework just as well.

Often, the social life of students revolves around fraternity parties, and on some campuses, institutions provide few alternatives. Fraternity parties can become a model for students' social life, i.e., large group functions with alcohol, loud music, although in some instances they may lead to vandalism and sexual abuse. The evidence is startling: reports from some campuses indicate that at least a few fraternities have actually planned a "gang bang" as part of a weekend's activities.

THE ROLE OF ALCOHOL AND DRUGS IN GANG RAPES

Alcohol and/or drugs are almost always involved in campus gang rape incidents. Although not a direct cause of rape, the mood-altering effects of these substances apparently help to set the stage by reducing men's inhibitions and helping them excuse or rationalize their abusive behavior. It affects a woman's ability to assess dangerous situations and also lessens her capacity to take effective steps to safeguard herself.

A woman's use of alcohol or drugs, however, may implicate her in the eyes of others as an "accessory" to the crime or at least a "willing participant." Again, she is held accountable for what happened to her despite the fact that she was participating in the same drinking behavior as the men. Men can drink with their friends and not worry about being taken advantage of. They are not victimized by their friends and peers— they are not raped, sodomized, or otherwise violated. Women who drink do not have that luxury. If a woman should become drunk at a fraternity or other campus party, the men at the party have several options: they can choose to ignore her, they can help her, or they can exploit her. At too many college parties, the men are choosing to take advantage of her.

Many fraternities glorify drinking and may deliberately encourage women to overdrink. At one institution, members of one fraternity kept a chart that listed the number of beers it took to seduce certain women. On some campuses, only alcohol is served at fraternity parties; no other beverage is available. Campus control of alcohol at parties is often inadequate or absent. However, a growing number of colleges and universities are proposing and enforcing stricter regulations regarding the use of alcohol on campus. Many are also developing programs to deal with students' abuse of alcohol.

HOW TO PREVENT CAMPUS GANG RAPE

Unlike stranger-to-stranger rape prevention programs discussed earlier in this chapter, the potential victim has considerable control over avoiding those situations where she can become the victim of a gang rape. It appears quite clear that there is a direct link between alcohol, drugs and gang rape. If a woman chooses to use alcohol or drugs in a social setting when there are men present, she must be constantly on her guard. If she overindulges, her judgment and decision-making powers will be affected and she can be easily victimized.

It is true that many colleges and universities have highly developed programs for handling such incidents after they occur, but in the final analysis prevention is the best course of action.[6]

SUGGESTED CAMPUS SECURITY QUESTIONS

The following list of questions is intended to assist both students and college administrators in evaluating the quality and quantity of the college rape prevention efforts and programs.

1. Does the campus have a rape awareness/crime prevention program for faculty, staff and students? If yes, how is it publicized?
2. Are campus police/security officers trained in rape prevention and investigation?
3. What is the number of police/security officers on campus? How does that compare with campuses with similar-sized campuses in similar locations?
4. How many rapes or sex-related criminal incidents occurred on campus within the last 12 months? How does that compare with the year before? How does that compare with similar-sized campuses in similar locations?
4. Is the campus periodically surveyed in terms of identifying and correcting security hazards? (e.g., poor lights, locks, grounds maintenance)
6. Who is responsible for ensuring security deficiencies are corrected? Is this process documented?
7. Are isolated areas of campus such as parking lots and laundry rooms well lit? How frequently are these areas patrolled?
8. Does the campus have a "date rape" prevention program?
9. Does the campus provide counseling programs for students, faculty or staff who have been sexually or physically assaulted?
10. Does the campus have an escort service to assist persons concerned about walking alone on campus?
11. Does the campus police/security department have women on their staff to assist in rape investigations?

12. Are campus high-risk areas identified and subsequently patrolled more frequently?
13. Are emergency phones available on campus?
14. Who may access campus dorms after the hours of darkness? Are dorm keys restricted? Are exterior dorm doors kept locked after dark?
15. Is crime prevention/personal safety material made available to the campus population?
16. Is the campus police department made aware of sexual assaults occurring adjacent to campus? Is this information shared with the campus community?
17. How many incidents of gang rape have been reported to campus officials within the last 12 months?
18. Were alcohol or drugs involved in any of the gang or date rapes reported?
19. If assailants were identified in gang rapes, what discipline or form of criminal charges were invoked?
20. Are gang or date rapes investigated formally by campus law enforcement or if necessary by local police?
21. Does the campus have a date or gang rape policy which is publicized to all campus groups?
22. Are victims of date or gang rapes provided professional counseling?
23. Are fraternities, sororities, residence hall groups and other student organizations provided information relating to the campus police regarding date and gang rape behavior? Are legal implications discussed as well?
24. Are men also invited to campus rape preventions programs?
25. Are academic classes used as forums for date or gang rape presentations?
26. Is a campus counseling center "hot line" available to rape victims?
27. Are campus law enforcement officials made aware when large-scale campus parties are scheduled in order to make periodic checks?

REFERENCES

1. C.R. Swanson, N.C. Chamelin, and L. Territo. *Criminal Investigation,* 4th ed. New York: McGraw-Hill, 1988, p. 317.
2. *Rape and Acquaintance Rape for Men and Women.* Vanderbilt University, Department of Police and Security, Nashville, TN, 1988.

3. *Sexual Assault,* Office of the Attorney General, Tallahassee, FL, 1978.

4. *Avoiding Acquaintance Rape for Men and Women,* Rochester Institute of Technology, Rochester, NY, 1988.

5. Julie K. Ehrhart and Bernice Sandler, "Campus Gang Rape: Legal Liability." In Leonard Territo and Max L. Bromley (Eds.), *Hospital and College Security Liability.* Columbia, MD: Hanrow Press, 1987.

6. Ibid., pp. 211–212.

Chapter 6

PROTECTING STUDENT
PROPERTY AND VEHICLES ON CAMPUS

One of the most frequently reported crimes on campus is theft of student property, and the majority of investigations of these thefts reveal no signs of forced entry into dorm rooms, cars and so forth. The reason is very simple: the student went off and left his or her dorm or car unlocked. The first recommendation thus is a very simple one. Students should lock their doors each time they leave their dorms or vehicles, even if they plan to be away for a short period of time. In the case of theft from dorm rooms, a substantial number occur during the lunch hour when rooms are left unsecured. If a room is locked, there is less opportunity for crimes to occur. For any type of crime to occur two elements must be present: the opportunity and the desire. We obviously have little control over the desire of others to commit crimes, but we certainly have a great deal of control over their ability to commit the crime. Thus, some simple preventive actions can eliminate the opportunity for a theft to occur.

Some thefts from dorm rooms are committed by friends, hallmates, or visitors to the dorm. Students, in particular, often become lulled into believing their peers are all truthworthy and they fail to safeguard property in their new and relaxed university setting. Students must recognize the importance of properly securing their belongings. Wallets, purses, wristwatches, calculators, and other items of value must not be left exposed on desks or dressers. They must be kept out of sight and, if possible, in a locked area such as a closet or drawer. Valuables should never be left unattended in common rooms where they are visible to others.

BURGLARY ON CAMPUS

Another serious crime on college campuses occurring frequently is burglary, which is typically the forceable entry into a dormitory room. If a student should return to a dorm room and finds signs of forcible entry, the room should not be entered. The police should be called immediately. Although burglary is a crime against property, there is a high potential for personal injury if the victim surprises the burglar. If a student is awakened inside his or her room, they should not try to apprehend the intruder but instead pretend to be asleep if there is no immediate danger. If there is some danger and if the opportunity presents itself, the student should try to leave as quickly and safely as possible. Students should never go to sleep with doors unlocked.

Many students use memo boards on their dorm room doors. When away from their rooms, they should never leave a note stating their absence or anticipated time of return. Such information gives criminals a time frame in which to work.[1]

OPERATION IDENTIFICATION

Many college campus security departments have a program designated as OPERATION IDENTIFICATION. Such programs are intended to mark personal property in such a way so that first it can be positively identified as belonging to a specific person and, second, if stolen and recovered, can be traced back to the owner. These two objectives are accomplished as follows:

First, the property is identified by engraving a set of numbers on it which will make it possible to trace it back to the owner if recovered by the police.

Second, a sticker is displayed that lets the potential thief know in advance that the property has been marked for identification purposes (see Figure 6-1).

Engraving Your Property

The engravers typically used are capable of marking steel, plastic, glass, wood, or any hard surface. The identifying number most often recommended by the police for engraving on property is a driver's license. Police agencies across the country have access to these numbers through state motor vehicle records. It is not recommended that a social security number be used because of the difficulty the police have in getting identifying information from the Social Security Administration. The number should not be engraved on an area that can be easily dismantled. Naturally, the item's own serial number can be used for identification later on if an accurate record of this number has been kept.

If the serial number is on a peel-off label, then it should be re-engraved on the item. When an object is engraved with a driver's license number, a letter should be added to it. An example of how this can be done is identified in Figure 6-2.

Any additional items that are engraved would get the next item letter in the sequence (e.g., DE1234567-B, DE1234567-C) and it would continue in this order). If there are more items to mark than letters in the alphabet, one should begin again using letters AA through ZZ. The

Figure 6-1.

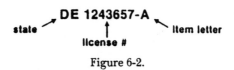

Figure 6-2.

letters are required by the FBI so that if the item is ever stolen it will have a unique number for entry into the National Crime Information Center.[2]

After property is marked, a list of the valuables should be made and a copy of the list kept in a safe place. If a theft occurs, the victim will be able to quickly describe the stolen property from the list. This will be of great help to the police in their attempts to recover the stolen property. When property has been marked and a list made, an OPERATION IDENTIFICATION sticker may be displayed on doors and/or windows which might be used for entry. By advertising one's participation in OPERATION IDENTIFICATION, they are announcing that their valuable property has been marked and will be difficult for burglars to resell. Often, the presence of the sticker alone is enough to deter a burglar.

Possessions To Be Marked

- TV sets
- Stereo equipment
- Guns
- Radios
- Car tape decks
- Tape recorders
- Fishing rods, reels
- Vacuum cleaners
- Kitchen appliances (e.g., mixers, toasters)
- Typewriters
- Adding machines
- Dictating machines
- Cameras
- Binoculars
- Hubcaps
- Mag wheels
- CB radios
- Golf clubs
- Electric shavers
- Watches
- Clocks
- Bicycles

BICYCLE THEFT

Many bicycles are no longer the relatively inexpensive recreational and transportation vehicles that they were several years ago. Many are worth hundreds of dollars and are often the target of thieves. In some cases, the thieves come on campus specifically to steal these expensive bicycles. Many of the bikes that are stolen had been left unsecured outside dormitories and other campus buildings for "just a few minutes." Bicycles, like any other property, should be kept locked up at all times.

Many campus police departments have bicycle registration programs. This free service often includes affixing a sticker and stamping the owner's driver's license number under the frame and filing a record of the make, model, and serial number of the bike. Other recommendations include:

- Always secure the bike (preferably both wheels and frame) to an immovable object.
- Use U-locks such as kryptonite or citadel locks. If a cable or chain lock is preferred, it should be at least 3/8″ in diameter with a pad lock of equal strength.
- Lock the vehicle in a well-lit, frequently traveled area.
- Notify the police department immediately if the bike is stolen.

PROTECTING CARS AGAINST THIEVES

There is quite likely no item of personal property that a student will have on campus that is of greater value than his or her automobile, and, therefore, it makes good sense to do everything possible to protect it and the accessories from would-be thieves. Auto thieves generally fall into four categories. The first is the joyrider who is typically a teenager between the ages of 15 to 19 who steals the car just for the sheer thrill of stealing it or on a dare. It may even be as an initiation into a gang or, occasionally, sometimes for the parts and accessories. The second type of thief is someone who will steal a car for use in other crimes. This type of thief will steal a car and abandon it immediately after the crime so that it cannot be traced to them. The third type of thief is someone who will steal a car for transportation. When they arrive at their destination, they will frequently abandon the vehicle. If they run out of gas before reaching their destination, they may abandon it at that time also. The last type of thief is the professional thief who steals a car for the purpose of altering it for resale or cannibalizing it and selling the parts.[3]

AUTO THEFT PREVENTION

There is much that can be done to make it more difficult for a thief to steal a car. For example:

1. Never leave a car unlocked, even for a few minutes.
2. Never leave the keys in the ignition.
3. Do not leave a car unlocked or unattended while loading and unloading personal items.
4. Do not leave articles exposed in the car when it is unattended. Place valuables in the trunk.
5. Park only in well-lighted areas and, whenever possible, in monitored, limited-access garages and lots. Avoid parking near shrubbery or trees, which could conceal potential attackers.
6. Check the car very carefully before entering, with a critical eye for possible break-ins or persons hiding in the rear seat or on the floor.
7. If the car is parked off campus in a commercial parking lot that requires the car keys to be left, only the ignition key should be left behind. If the trunk key is left, there is a possibility of losing every item in the trunk. If house keys are left, a potentially dishonest parking lot attendant could make duplicate keys and then later use them to break into the car owner's apartment or home.
8. Record and keep in a safe location the following information:
   - Make and model
   - Model year
   - Registration number
   - Color
   - Vehicle identification number
   - Engine size
   - Any peculiarities your car may have including dents, pinstripes, etc.
   - The name of your insurance company and agent

ANTI-THEFT DEVICES

There are a number of anti-theft devices that can be installed in the car which will make it much more difficult for potential thieves. The following are some examples.

- First is a kill switch—a simple and inexpensive device which when used cuts off the auto's electrical system without which the ignition circuitry is incomplete and the car cannot be started.
- Fuel switch—closes a valve that cuts off the fuel supply.
- Armored collar—a metal shield that locks around the steering column and covers the ignition to prevent the ignition from being tampered with.
- Crock lock—a hook-shaped bar which locks the steering wheel to the brake pedal.
- Alarm system—loud warning alarm sounds an alert if the car is tampered with or jostled.
- Coil wire—you can disable your own car by removing the coil wire which runs from the center of the distributor cap to the top plate of the coil. No tools are required for removal.
- Door locks—replace cap-type locks with tamper proof door locks. This helps combat the thief with a coat hanger.[4]

ADDITIONAL ANTI–THEFT TIPS

- Consider special locks for easy-to-steal parts such as wire wheels, gas caps, and seats. A hood lock will help protect the battery and engine parts.
- Borrow an engraving tool from the campus police and put the driver's license number on such items as tape decks, CB's, and hubcaps.
- Mount CB's, tape decks and scanners out of sight if possible. Use slide-in and slide-out mounting and portable antennaes for easy removal. Remove them when the car is unoccupied or lock them in the trunk of the vehicle.

SELF-ASSESSMENT SECURITY QUESTIONS

The following list of questions are intended to assist students in assessing how well they are protecting their property from potential thieves.

1. Are dorm rooms, offices or apartments locked when the occupant's are going to be away from it for any period of time?
2. Are valuables such as wallets, purses, wristwatches, and calculators kept out of sight whenever possible and in a locked area such as a closet or drawer?
3. When a dorm room occupant is going to be away from the room for any period of time, do they use message boards and advise would-be visitors how long they will be gone and when they are expected to return?
4. If the college has an OPERATION IDENTIFICATION program, has the student marked all of his or her property with their driver's license number and kept a record of this information in a safe place?
5. Are bicycles always kept secure when unattended even for a few minutes?
6. Are car keys ever left in the ignition and then the car left unattended even for a few minutes?
7. Are articles left exposed in the car when it is unattended?
8. Is the vehicle parked in well-lighted areas whenever possible, and does the driver avoid parking near shrubs, trees and other places that would conceal would-be attackers?
9. Is the interior of the car examined before entering it to be sure that no one is hiding in it?
10. When a car is left at a commercial parking lot, is only the ignition key left while removing all other keys such as trunk keys and house keys?
11. Have anti-theft devices been installed in the car?

ENDNOTES

1. *Crime Prevention.* Nashville, TN: Vanderbilt University, 1988, p. 12.
2. *You Can Help Stop Theft.* University of Delaware, Department of Public Safety, 1988, p. 2.
3. C.R. Swanson, N.C. Chamelin, and L. Territo, *Criminal Investigation*, 4th ed. New York: McGraw-Hill, 1988, pp. 410–412.
4. *Auto Theft.* Cambridge, MA: Massachusetts Institute of Technology, 1988, p. 2.

INDEX